1980s Project Studies/Council on Foreign Relations

STUDIES AVAILABLE

CHALLENGES TO INTERDEPENDENT ECONOMIES
The Industrial West in the Coming Decade
Studies by Robert J. Gordon and Jacques Pelkmans

SHARING GLOBAL RESOURCES
Studies by Ruth W. Arad and Uzi B. Arad, Rachel McCulloch and José Piñera, and Ann L. Hollick

AFRICA IN THE 1980s:
A Continent in Crisis
Studies by Colin Legum, I. William Zartman, and Steven Langdon and Lynn K. Mytelka

ENHANCING GLOBAL HUMAN RIGHTS
Studies by Jorge I. Domínguez, Nigel S. Rodley, Bryce Wood, and Richard Falk

OIL POLITICS IN THE 1980s:
Patterns of International Cooperation
Øystein Noreng

SIX BILLION PEOPLE:
Demographic Dilemmas and World Politics
Studies by Georges Tapinos and Phyllis T. Piotrow

THE MIDDLE EAST IN THE COMING DECADE:
From Wellhead to Well-being?
Studies by John Waterbury and Ragaei El Mallakh

REDUCING GLOBAL INEQUITIES
Studies by W. Howard Wriggins and Gunnar Adler-Karlsson

RICH AND POOR NATIONS IN THE WORLD ECONOMY
Studies by Albert Fishlow, Carlos F. Díaz-Alejandro, Richard R. Fagen, and Roger D. Hansen

CONTROLLING FUTURE ARMS TRADE

Studies by Anne Hessing Cahn and Joseph J. Kruzel, Peter M. Dawkins, and Jacques Huntzinger

DIVERSITY AND DEVELOPMENT IN SOUTHEAST ASIA:

The Coming Decade

Studies by Guy J. Pauker, Frank H. Golay, and Cynthia H. Enloe

NUCLEAR WEAPONS AND WORLD POLITICS:

Alternatives for the Future

Studies by David C. Gompert, Michael Mandelbaum, Richard L. Garwin, and John H. Barton

CHINA'S FUTURE:

Foreign Policy and Economic Development in the Post-Mao Era

Studies by Allen S. Whiting and Robert F. Dernberger

ALTERNATIVES TO MONETARY DISORDER

Studies by Fred Hirsch and Michael W. Doyle and by Edward L. Morse

NUCLEAR PROLIFERATION:

Motivations, Capabilities, and Strategies for Control

Studies by Ted Greenwood and by Harold A. Feiveson and Theodore B. Taylor

INTERNATIONAL DISASTER RELIEF:

Toward a Responsive System

Stephen Green

STUDIES FORTHCOMING

The 1980s Project will comprise about 25 volumes. Most will contain independent but related studies concerning issues of potentially great importance in the next decade and beyond, such as resource management, human rights, population studies, and relations between the developing and developed societies, among many others. Additionally, a number of volumes will be devoted to particular regions of the world, concentrating especially on political and economic development trends outside the industrialized West.

Challenges to Interdependent Economies

Challenges to Interdependent Economies

THE INDUSTRIAL WEST IN THE COMING DECADE

ROBERT J. GORDON

JACQUES PELKMANS

Introduction by Edward L. Morse and Thomas Wallin

1980s Project/Council on Foreign Relations

McGRAW-HILL BOOK COMPANY

New York   St. Louis   San Francisco
Auckland   Bogotá   Düsseldorf   Johannesburg   London   Madrid
Mexico   Montreal   New Delhi   Panama   Paris   São Paulo
Singapore   Sydney   Tokyo   Toronto

The Council on Foreign Relations, Inc., is a nonprofit and nonpartisan organization devoted to promoting improved understanding of international affairs through the free exchange of ideas. Its membership of about 1,700 persons throughout the United States is made up of individuals with special interest and experience in international affairs. The Council has no affiliation with and receives no funding from the United States government.

The Council publishes the journal *Foreign Affairs* and, from time to time, books and monographs that in the judgment of the Council's Committee on Studies are responsible treatments of significant international topics worthy of presentation to the public. The 1980s Project is a research effort of the Council; as such, 1980s Project Studies have been similarly reviewed through procedures of the Committee on Studies. As in the case of all Council publications, statements of fact and expressions of opinion contained in 1980s Project Studies are the sole responsibility of their authors.

The editor of this book was Thomas Wallin for the Council on Foreign Relations. Thomas Quinn and Michael Hennelly were the editors for McGraw-Hill Book Company. Christopher Simon was the designer, and Teresa Leaden supervised the production. This book was set in Times Roman by Offset Composition Services, Inc.

Printed and bound by R. R. Donnelley and Sons.

Library of Congress Cataloging in Publication Data

Gordon, Robert J.
Challenges to interdependent economies.

(1980s Project/Council on Foreign Relations)
Bibliography: p.
Includes index.
1. United States—Economic policy—1971–
2. International economic relations. 3. Economic
history—1945– I. Pelkmans, Jacques, joint author.
II. Title. III. Series: Council on Foreign Relations.
1980s Project/Council on Foreign Relations.
HC106.7.G67   330.9′73′092   78-13407
ISBN 0-07-023810-3
ISBN 0-07-023811-1 pbk.

1 2 3 4 5 6 7 8 9 R R D R R D 7 9 8 0 3 2 1 0 9

Contents

Foreword: The 1980s Project

The sluggishness of economic growth and the persistence of both inflation and unemployment in the Western industrial countries have posed trenchant questions about the economic theory of demand management and the political ability of governments to coordinate their domestic economic policies. The essays in this volume focus upon both the theoretical and practical political issues raised by the recession of the second half of the 1970s and their implications for international relations in the coming decade. They are part of a stream of studies that have grown out of the 1980s Project of the Council on Foreign Relations, each of which analyzes issues that are likely to be of international concern during the next 10 to 20 years.

The ambitious purpose of the 1980s Project is to examine important political and economic problems not only individually but in relationship to one another. Some studies or books produced by the Project will primarily emphasize the interrelationship of issues. In the case of other, more specifically focused studies, a considerable effort has been made to write, review, and criticize them in the context of more general Project work. Each Project study is thus capable of standing on its own; at the same time it has been shaped by a broader perspective.

The 1980s Project had its origin in the widely held recognition that many of the assumptions, policies, and institutions that have characterized international relations during the past 30 years are inadequate to the demands of today and the foreseeable demands of the period between now and 1990 or so. Over the course of the next decade, substantial adaptation of institutions and behavior will be needed to respond to the changed circumstances of the 1980s and beyond. The Project seeks to identify those future conditions and the kinds of adaptation they might require. It is not the Project's purpose to arrive at a single or exclusive set of goals. Nor does it focus upon the foreign policy or national interests of the United States alone. Instead, it seeks to identify goals that are compatible with the perceived interests of most states, despite differences in ideology and in level of economic development.

The published products of the Project are aimed at a broad readership, including policy makers and potential policy makers and those who would influence the policy-making process, but are confined to no single nation or region. The authors of Project studies were therefore asked to remain mindful of interests broader than those of any one society and to take fully into account the likely realities of domestic politics in the principal societies involved. All those who have worked on the Project, however, have tried not to be captives of the status quo; they have sought to question the inevitability of existing patterns of thought and behavior that restrain desirable change and to look for ways in which those patterns might in time be altered or their consequences mitigated.

The 1980s Project is at once a series of separate attacks upon a number of urgent and potentially urgent international problems and also a collective effort, involving a substantial number of persons in the United States and abroad, to bring those separate approaches to bear upon one another and to suggest the kinds of choices that might be made among them. The Project involves more than 300 participants. A small central staff and a steering Coordinating Group have worked to define the questions and to assess the compatibility of policy prescriptions. Nearly 100 authors, from more than a dozen countries, have been at work on separate studies. Ten working groups of specialists and generalists have been convened to subject the Project's studies to critical scrutiny and to help in the process of identifying interrelationships among them.

The 1980s Project is the largest single research and studies effort the Council on Foreign Relations has undertaken in its 55-year history, comparable in conception only to a major study of the postwar world, the War and Peace Studies, undertaken by the Council during the Second World War. At that time, the impetus of the effort was the discontinuity caused by worldwide conflict and the visible and inescapable need to rethink, replace, and supplement many of the features of the international system that had prevailed before the war. The discontinuities in today's world are less obvious and, even when occasionally quite visible—as in the abandonment of gold convertibility and fixed monetary parities—only briefly command the spotlight of public attention. That new institutions and patterns of behavior are needed in many areas is widely acknowledged, but the sense of need is less urgent—existing institutions have not for the most part dramatically failed and collapsed. The tendency, therefore, is to make do with outmoded arrangements and to improvise rather than to undertake a basic analysis of the problems that lie before us and of the demands that those problems will place upon all nations.

The 1980s Project is based upon the belief that serious effort and integrated forethought can contribute—indeed, are indispensable—to progress in the next decade toward a more humane, peaceful, productive, and just world. And it rests upon the hope that participants in its deliberations and readers of Project publications—whether or not they agree with an author's point of view—may be helped to think more informedly about the opportunities and the dangers that lie ahead and the consequences of various possible courses of future action.

The 1980s Project has been made possible by generous grants from the Ford Foundation, the Lilly Endowment, the Andrew W. Mellon Foundation, the Rockefeller Foundation, and the German Marshall Fund of the United States. Neither the Council on Foreign Relations nor any of those foundations is responsible for statements of fact and expressions of opinion contained in publications of the 1980s Project; they are the sole responsibility of the individual authors under whose names they appear. But the

Council on Foreign Relations and the staff of the 1980s Project take great pleasure in placing those publications before a wide readership both in the United States and abroad.

The 1980s Project

1980s PROJECT WORKING GROUPS

During 1975 and 1976, ten Working Groups met to explore major international issues and to subject initial drafts of 1980s Project studies to critical review. Those who chaired Project Working Groups were:

Cyrus R. Vance, Working Group on Nuclear Weapons and Other Weapons of Mass Destruction

Leslie H. Gelb, Working Group on Armed Conflict

Roger Fisher, Working Group on Transnational Violence and Subversion

Rev. Theodore M. Hesburgh, Working Group on Human Rights

Joseph S. Nye, Jr., Working Group on the Political Economy of North-South Relations

Harold Van B. Cleveland, Working Group on Macroeconomic Policies and International Monetary Relations

Lawrence C. McQuade, Working Group on Principles of International Trade

William Diebold, Jr., Working Group on Multinational Enterprises

Eugene B. Skolnikoff, Working Group on the Environment, the Global Commons, and Economic Growth

Miriam Camps, Working Group on Industrial Policy

1980s PROJECT STAFF

Persons who have held senior professional positions on the staff of the 1980s Project for all or part of its duration are:

Miriam Camps	*Catherine Gwin*
William Diebold, Jr.	*Roger D. Hansen*
Tom J. Farer	*Edward L. Morse*
David C. Gompert	*Richard H. Ullman*

Richard H. Ullman was Director of the 1980s Project from its inception in 1974 until July 1977, when he became Chairman of the Project Coordinating Group. Edward L. Morse was Executive Director from July 1977 until June 1978. At that time, Catherine Gwin, 1980s Project Fellow since 1976, took over as Executive Director.

PROJECT COORDINATING GROUP

The Coordinating Group of the 1980s Project had a central advisory role in the work of the Project. Its members as of June 30, 1978, were:

Carlos F. Díaz-Alejandro
Richard A. Falk
Tom J. Farer
Edward K. Hamilton
Stanley Hoffmann
Gordon J. MacDonald
Bruce K. MacLaury

Bayless Manning
Theodore R. Marmor
Ali Mazrui
Michael O'Neill
Stephen Stamas
Fritz Stern
Allen S. Whiting

Until they entered government service, other members included:

W. Michael Blumenthal
Richard N. Cooper
Samuel P. Huntington

Joseph S. Nye, Jr.
Marshall D. Shulman

COMMITTEE ON STUDIES

The Committee on Studies of the Board of Directors of the Council on Foreign Relations is the governing body of the 1980s Project. The Committee's members as of June 30, 1978, were:

Barry E. Carter
Robert A. Charpie
Stanley Hoffmann
Henry A. Kissinger
Walter J. Levy

Robert E. Osgood
Stephen Stamas
Paul A. Volcker
Marina v. N. Whitman

James A. Perkins (Chairman)

Challenges to Interdependent Economies

Introduction: Demand Management and Economic Nationalism in the Coming Decade

Edward L. Morse and Thomas Wallin

The economic vitality of North America, Japan, and the European Community is critical to the shape of the 1980s. Without growth and prosperity in these key industrial countries, the health of the world economy will be endangered. The poorer members of the Organization for Economic Cooperation and Development (OECD), the petroleum-exporting countries, the rest of the less developed nations, and even the planned economies depend in varying degrees on the economic strength of the advanced industrial societies. If they falter, the next decade could be a period of global economic contraction or perhaps depression, generating political tensions both domestically and internationally.

In the long run, the economic vitality of these key Western countries depends largely on their economic growth; in the short run, it lies in the success of their macroeconomic policies: those dealing with the general level of prices and employment, economic activity, and the overall stability of the economy. This is not to deny the significance of the behavior of individual firms and consumers or the relationship of governments to basic economic actors and sectors; but in terms of the welfare of the entire society, it is the economy as a whole that is most important. After a period of unprecedented growth and stability in the key industrial nations during the two decades following World War II, the world economy entered a period of uncertainty. Economic interdependence has increasingly required a stronger effort by the largest Western countries to coordinate their domestic de-

1

mand management policies, lest the actions of some contradict those of others. The uneven experience of the 1970s has taught us to be skeptical of the ability of governments effectively to make and coordinate macroeconomic policies. One manifestation of this uncertainty is that macroeconomic policies no longer stand on firm ground—in terms of either theoretical analysis or recent experiences.

Past prosperity can be attributed in large measure to the success of domestic demand management and international economic integration. The leadership of the United States, the progressive dismantling of trade barriers, and the depoliticization of international economic affairs through the International Monetary Fund (IMF) and the General Agreement on Tariffs and Trade (GATT) provided a basis for expanding international commerce. Fiscal and monetary policy gave governments some control over the business cycle. Economic interdependence among the advanced industrial societies thrived in this atmosphere of economic stability and more open markets, and this fed into the processes of growth. Interdependence was a boon to all of them, providing economic gains far larger than any society could achieve on its own. And governments were generally able to provide a stable climate for investment and capital accumulation by the private sector. However, in the changing circumstances of the late 1960s and early 1970s, the viability of the system came into question.

The confidence of governments in their ability to control their domestic economies through fiscal and monetary policies increased during the first two decades after World War II. Evidence of their skill can be seen in the declining volatility of the business cycle during these years. However, by the 1970s the leading Western economies were in disarray. The rates of inflation and unemployment that prevailed in the 1960s had tripled. The mid-1970s brought the worst recession of the postwar period, and this setback continues to hamper growth in many leading industrial countries. The loss of confidence in macroeconomic policy making was both a cause and an effect of the recession. It combined with various objective factors in producing the slowdown, and the severity of the economic crisis itself added to the feeling

2

that the methods of demand management were flawed. This can be seen at the theoretical level in the fact that economists continue to be as perplexed with "stagflation" as they were before the recession. As a structural problem, it remains without any clear solution.

At the international level, the volume of international transactions increased and the economic openness of societies expanded to the benefit of all. However, interdependence cuts two ways. The growth in market integration provided the leading Western nations with tremendous economic gains, but at the cost of greater national vulnerability. Economic shocks, such as currency speculation, oil-price increases, and changes in national macroeconomic policies are transmitted from country to country in an interdependent environment. This is precisely what happened during the recession, compounding the strains of domestic economic contraction and limiting the ability of governments to respond to the crisis. The process of economic integration has thus complicated the task of governments in producing effective macroeconomic policies.

The recession of the mid-1970s clearly points out the dilemma that stagflation and the complexities of economic interdependence pose for the 1980s. Production and distribution have become internationalized over the last 30 years and, at the same time, they continue to be critical determinants of social and political stability. In general terms, the cause of the problem is that successful demand management involves a constant tension between short-term and long-term priorities. The need to respond to short-run disturbances often requires governments to pursue policies that have destructive consequences later on. The clearest example of this can be seen in electoral politics. The governments of the leading industrial states know that unless they provide their electorates with a stable and prosperous economic environment, they are likely to lose power, and yet some of the most politically attractive means to achieve these goals—import quotas, export subsidies, aggressive exchange-rate intervention and so forth—are potentially destructive to the international economic system and to themselves. As a result, governments, acting to preserve their economic gains, often end up pursuing

3

policies that can harm other societies as well as their own. This situation in essence creates a new form of economic nationalism. It is an expression of national frustration and defensiveness in the face of the apparent failure of the twin pistons of Western economic prosperity, international market integration and successful macroeconomic management.

The studies in this volume are responses to the problems of macroeconomic management and the new economic nationalism. They describe origins and elements of different aspects of these problems in complementary ways. However, their conclusions differ, reflecting the range of positions that exist on these questions and underlining some of the issues that are likely to be important in the next decade.

Robert J. Gordon, professor of economics at Northwestern University in Illinois, studies the problems of domestic macroeconomic policy in the United States. He clarifies the basic debate in economic theory between the "monetarist" and "nonmonetarist" schools of thought and suggests how the United States economy could look in the next decade according to various combinations of policy measures. He addressses some of the international implications of macroeconomic policies, but is primarily concerned with the performance of the United States economy. He assumes that, with the exception of oil imports, the United States can be considered essentially a closed economy.

Others, especially Europeans, point to the increasing openness of the American economy, not only to oil but also to imports of machinery and manufactured goods from OECD nations. This economic openness is also apparent in the growing amount of direct foreign investment in the United States. In sum, they see the United States as becoming vulnerable to outside pressures in much the same way that other OECD nations are. As a consequence of greater economic openness the effectiveness of US demand management becomes contingent on the policy choices of other OECD members. This perspective emphasizes the need for macroeconomic policy coordination. It is, at least in part, the point of departure of the final essay in this volume.

The essay by Jacques Pelkmans, a professor of economics at Tilburg University in the Netherlands, analyzes international economic cooperation. Pelkmans looks at the role of domestic politics in the interdependent economic relations of the advanced industrial countries, which are at the heart of the new economic nationalism. He then sets up a framework for understanding the different types of cooperation that have existed and could exist among these countries. He concludes with an examination of the types of cooperation that might be desirable and feasible in the 1980s.

In good Socratic form, these essays raise questions that not only point to the limitations of our knowledge about the new economic nationalism but also underline issues that are vital for our understanding of the next decade. Some of these issues are new and some are old, but there is no doubt that they will dominate thinking about the international implications of macro-economic policy. In what follows we discuss the roots and distinctive features of the new economic nationalism, explore the broad spectrum of problems that arise in policy cooperation, and offer some policy guidelines for forging collective leadership among the key Western economies.

THE NEW ECONOMIC NATIONALISM

Unlike the economic nationalism of the 1930s or the mercantilism and colonial imperialism of the past, economic nationalism today does not place the highest priority on increasing one state's power or wealth at the expense of others'. On the contrary, the new economic nationalism is born of anxiety rather than opportunity, but like its predecessors, it, too, has the potential for politicizing economic relations. It is motivated by the fear of economic vulnerability to processes that are poorly understood and seem to originate abroad. If the politicization of international economic issues, which grows out of this fear, is to be curbed and reduced to manageable proportions, one must first understand its roots.

As Pelkmans argues, a major factor in the reappearance of economic nationalism is the importance governments place on autonomy in national economic policy making. Autonomy allows governments to achieve the objectives of the welfare state even in the face of the adverse consequences of international interdependence, which are most keenly felt in periods of contraction. Elected officials feel that autonomy provides them with better control over the outcomes of market processes and the objectives of their discretionary expenditures. Modern capitalist societies desire, in short, to reduce both market and policy interdependencies in order to restrict the consequences and thus improve governmental control over the domestic economy.

This emphasis on autonomy predates the recession of the 1970s, but in nonrecessionary periods it is curbed and balanced to a large degree by the benefits of interdependence with economic partners, which provide not only trade gains but also a larger effective tax base for certain redistributive policies. This has traditionally been a significant factor for each member of the European Community in its quest for greater integration. While German society and business gained by producing for a larger effective market, Italians benefited from Community-financed development projects, and France prospered because of the commonly funded agricultural policy. In periods of economic growth, not only is the quest for autonomy offset by gains from economic openness, but each individual country's search for specific domestic benefits can be traded off with others' through international negotiations.

The tension between the pursuit of domestic gains through international means on the one hand and through national autonomy on the other hand is exacerbated by two related factors. First, as we have seen, recession tilts the balance clearly toward reliance on national unilateral measures. Second, to the degree that national policy is oriented toward structural—as opposed to cyclical—factors, the balance seems to be weighted heavily toward unilateral national measures. And while an analytical separation can be drawn between longer-term structural problems and shorter-term cyclical ones, in practice this distinction is almost impossible to make.[1]

---

[1] See William Diebold's forthcoming 1980s Project study on international industrial policies, in which the problem of separating cyclical from structural issues is dealt with in greater detail.

Cyclical problems can theoretically be distinguished from structural problems in terms of their causes and their likely duration. They relate to shifts in prices, employment levels, and prevailing exchange rates caused by temporary changes in effective demand. Structural problems are also manifested in problems of price stability and employment levels, but they are more deeply rooted than cyclical problems and related to such issues as the size and structure of the labor market and industry, patterns of capital accumulation and investment, and the international competitiveness of tradable goods produced in a society. Long-term structural issues are often exacerbated by short-term cyclical phenomena. In recent years, for example, structural problems of overcapacity in such industries as steel, automobiles, textiles and fibers, and shipbuilding were worsened by the simultaneity of the cyclical recession in the industrialized countries. And the effort by some countries to reduce overcapacity through unilateral measures such as price cutting on the international markets reduced the ability of net importing countries to deal with their own cyclical problems.

The blurred distinction between cyclical and structural problems is central to difficulties confronted by governments in their efforts to manage the international economy in order to maximize growth and restrict economic nationalism. In theory, cyclical and structural issues should be treated separately, and in the international coordination of policies this implies an emphasis on short-term cyclical flows, with national policy alone being reserved for structural, longer-term "adjustment" policies. However, in reality, when it comes to making policy the distinction is more one of degree than of kind. Thus structural problems are likely to require increasing amounts of international cooperation if they are to be solved without recourse to disruptive unilateral measures. In practice the very existence of seemingly intractable stagflation indicates that both cyclical and structural issues are at play in problems of growth, inflation, unemployment, and exchange-rate instability.

The economies of the industrialized world seem to be confronting different mixes of structural and cyclical problems. The United States, for example, has confronted structural unem-

7

ployment for the past two and a half decades. But with the end of the post-World War II baby boom and decreasing numbers of persons entering the labor market, structural unemployment of skilled labor may come to an end in the United States in the coming decade, even if unemployment continues among the unskilled. At the same time, European countries will be trying to provide employment opportunities for a burgeoning flow of entrants into the labor market and will likely be confronting structural unemployment for the first time since World War II. The arrival of new cohorts of the postwar European baby boom into the labor market and of other entrants, including women, has, however, coincided with the deepest and longest postwar recession, which has made it politically difficult to separate structural from cyclical employment policies and problems. Furthermore, in both cases the structural problem with labor is not just one of the numbers of workers; it also involves the number of skilled workers and the unwillingness of people to take certain kinds of jobs. The important point to note here is that these conditions vary from country to country, creating different levels and types of structural unemployment.

Another aspect of the desire for economic unilateralism, which is directly related to the impulses of the welfare state and the efforts to cope with cyclical and structural problems, is the prominence of new priorities in the management of national economies. This trend is most obvious in Britain, but certainly not absent in other industrial societies. It is the tendency to substitute welfare and quality of life for efficiency as the first priorities in the management of domestic economic life. This tendency has a direct impact on international market integration, which has traditionally been advocated on the grounds of global economic efficiency. Mistrust of the ability of the market to assure a just allocation of resources, the desire to achieve environmental quality control, the politically felt need to satisfy the demands of powerful pressure groups, the goal of assuring regional balance in patterns of growth, and the tendencies of persons working in governmental/bureaucratic settings to expand their domain of decision making have all contributed to the decline in importance of efficiency criteria and thus have reduced the scope and desirability of international market integration.

While some societies have been able to achieve both welfare and efficiency criteria simultaneously, through an acceleration of economic productivity and international market integration, others have not. Whether this failure will, by itself, lead to a more economically nationalist world is open to debate. Sweden, for example, has until recently been able to pursue welfare goals without losing the benefits of economic growth and productivity. And even in the United Kingdom, efforts to cope with this alleged dilemma of "postindustrial" society by deregulating the economy will continue in what is now an experimental laboratory for the rest of the industrial world.

Other aspects of the new economic nationalism are much more traditional and relate to the continued attraction governments find in pursuing a current account surplus—or, in the aftermath of the oil-price increases, in avoiding the hot potato of a deficit that corresponds to the surpluses of some of the OPEC countries. In the late 1960s and early 1970s it was widely believed, especially in the United States, that the politicization of international trade issues, associated with the fact that not all countries could simultaneously achieve current account surpluses, would be reduced by movement toward a flexible exchange-rate regime. For a while in the mid-1970s political frictions associated with trading issues seemed to be substantially reduced by exchange-rate flexibility. But the subsequent inability of the major governments in the West to establish even a few rules on managing exchange rates and the drive to promote exports in order to combat unemployment and pay for oil imports resulted in greater politicization of both trade and payments issues.

Whether these more traditional aspects of economic nationalism can be curbed depends in large measure upon the ability of the major participants in the world economy to agree to rules of behavior in the handling of international monetary and commercial problems.[2] And such agreements themselves depend, in a circular fashion, on the ability of governments to overcome the recession of the 1970s. The tendency of governments to impose

[2]See Fred Hirsch, Michael W. Doyle, and Edward L. Morse, *Alternatives to Monetary Disorder*, McGraw-Hill for the Council on Foreign Relations/1980s Project, New York, 1977, for a discussion of some possible rules.

restrictions on imports or on capital flows or to subsidize exports in periods of economic difficulty is well known. In the past, economic nationalism has been contained by the countervailing benefits of increased commerce in periods of growth or by interest groups that identify themselves with a liberal international economy and are not hurt by cyclical fluctuations. Should the current economic crisis be prolonged, the neonationalist forces at work are likely to put more and more pressure on the loose "truce" that exists among the advanced industrial countries not to use disruptive unilateral measures.

PROBLEMS OF POLICY COORDINATION

Curbing economic nationalism, attaining the objectives of domestic demand management, and creating stable international conditions for longer-term growth are all dependent upon the ability of the major governments of the OECD to develop procedures for coordinating domestic policies. In short, they depend upon the capacity of the major governments to develop collective leadership.

But collective leadership will remain an empty phrase until a great deal of additional experimentation on policy coordination takes places. This experimentation is clearly necessary for political reasons. As governments are generally reluctant to relinquish their autonomy of action, they are unlikely to develop appropriate trust in each other unless they have more opportunities to improvise solutions to their shared problems of economic management. A slow evolution of common experience and perhaps the emergence of a measure of international common law are the best that one should expect at the present time in the development of collective leadership. Given this general context, we summarize under the several headings below some issues that are critical to the productive evolution of policy coordination.

1. "Negative" versus "Positive" Cooperation

Attempts to harmonize and coordinate policies can be understood in terms of Jacques Pelkmans' distinction between positive and negative cooperation. As opposed to positive cooperation, which involves agreement on targets to be achieved or instruments to be used, negative cooperation involves either the dismantling of obstacles to economic flows (e.g., border controls, such as quotas and tariffs, or internal measures, such as subsidies) or agreement not to impose new obstacles.

The history of economic cooperation has essentially involved the first sort of negative cooperation: the removal of obstacles to what can loosely be called economic integration. The tariff reductions under the GATT have produced perhaps the most successful and general attempt at this type of policy cooperation to date.

A second type of negative policy cooperation pertains to commitments not to raise barriers to international flows of goods and services or to the mobile factors of production, especially technology and capital. Pledges taken by OECD countries to avoid using tariffs as a means of dealing with balance-of-payments problems arising out of the increased deficits due to oil-price rises is an example of this form of negative cooperation. The refusal to impose such barriers is especially significant today, when governments, confronting deficits, inflation, and unemployment at home, would want to use border controls to limit their vulnerability to pressures from abroad.

However, neither form of negative cooperation is adequate to assure policy cooperation in the middle or long run. Unless buttressed by more positive forms of cooperation, negative forms carry with them the seeds of their own destruction. At best they represent short-term solutions for the achievement of governmental objectives. For example, negative cooperation through the removal of trade barriers leads almost automatically to economic integration. This adversely affects domestic groups that are not internationally competitive, and it makes hidden barriers to trade seem more significant. These effects and others having to do with economic openness politicize relations and in times of economic contraction create protectionist pressures. There is no reason to assume that the politicization of relations will necessarily lead to effective long-run cooperation and political integration. In fact, without the establishment of means for coping with common problems it seems likely that neomercantilist tendencies will prevail because a return to autonomy provides the only other means for handling these politicized issues.

2. Policy Goals and Policy Instruments

There is also an important difference between policy goals and policy instruments. Without entering the impossible conundrum of when means are ends and vice versa, it clearly makes a difference for governments whether they jointly target their goals or they simply agree about the use of certain policy tools. What is not clear on a theoretical level is when it makes sense to focus on the one as opposed to the other.

It is sometimes easier for governments to coordinate policies by focusing on certain broad objectives, such as reducing inflation below double-digit levels or aiming to achieve a targeted rate of unemployment. Fixing upon common targets allows governments to invoke those instruments—fiscal, monetary, or border controls—that each finds most suitable to its special circumstances. This seems to be the way the loose form of policy coordination has been working (to the degree that it has) among OECD countries. But there are often cases in which major disputes, sometimes of an ideological nature, emerge from any effort to target objectives.

In recent years it has become nearly impossible to achieve agreement on such issues as the causes of inflation or the principles of a proper international monetary system. Gordon's essay is directed at the resolution of such theoretical disputes and thus is an important step toward improved policy coordination. In the meantime, however, cooperation is probably facilitated best through the pursuit of proxy goals. When irreconcilable theoretical disputes impede the achievement of consensus on goals, focusing on instruments is often the only way to achieve a modicum of cooperation. Out of pragmatism, consensus on appropriate instruments to serve as proximate or proxy goals can be a solution, as governments jointly try to reach common ground. Indeed, reform of the monetary system seems to be proceeding along these lines. If, a decade from now, the major monetary powers begin jointly to target their exchange rates and support them, it will matter little whether one group calls the system a "managed float" and another calls it a "return to fixed rates."

3. The Scope for Policy Coordination

The potential scope for policy coordination in the 1980s depends to a large degree upon how severe both cyclical and structural problems will be and whether governments will be able to handle them separately. If structural problems predominate and if the border line between them and more cyclical issues remains fuzzy, governments of the advanced economies will probably have more difficulty in developing mechanisms to cope with problems of demand management. Conversely, if cyclical problems intensify and a crisis atmosphere is generated, governments may well find it mutually advantageous to deepen the scope of policy coordination. In either case, an examination of the scope of policy coordination gives us a clearer sense of future problems. It is important to note, however, that structural conditions and issues, while not the subject of this volume, are significant in that the types of policy coordination treated here are different from but affected by them.

Returning to the types of policy coordination that are likely to be appropriate for dealing with different levels of interdependence as they affect demand management, it might be useful to make a few distinctions related to the general level of economic interrelatedness, beginning with the simplest and least complex. Pelkmans treats this topic in a far more detailed way. Our purpose here is simply to underline what seem to us to be some key points that relate to the goal of collective leadership.

At the most rudimentary level, a modest amount of interrelatedness can be dealt with on a minimal basis by governments pooling information and, perhaps, undertaking the common evaluation of problems. This sort of policy cooperation has been under way since the early 1960s in the OECD Secretariat and especially within the OECD's Economic Policy Committee structure. These efforts include several types of activities, from the pooling of data on recent economic activities to the more important sharing of information concerning short-term policy plans.

When governments commit themselves to tell their principal economic partners what they plan to do over the coming quarter or half year, three important functions are served. First, each government is provided with an opportunity to evaluate the effects of its partners' policies on its own domestic economy and can adjust its own policies in light of this additional information. Second, each government has the opportunity to make its partners aware of problems that it might encounter as a result of the policies they are pursuing and, perhaps, if only to a small degree, each might then convince the partners to change policies. Finally and perhaps most important, the very act of submitting one's domestic policies to the scrutiny of other governments helps a government to rationalize and make much more coherent its own short-term economic targets. In short, it forces economic coordination at home, which is a prerequisite to economic coordination abroad.

Higher levels of interdependence require much more in the way of policy coordination, including harmonization—the elimination or reduction of inconsistencies in policy instruments adopted by each individual government—or standardization—the adoption of similar targets (e.g., for money supply) or instruments (e.g., the same kind of tax system). Whether the OECD countries have reached a level of economic integration that requires very much in the way of harmonization or standardization is an open question. The European Community seems to have reached this stage, as can be seen by some harmonization of taxation systems and some standardization of licensing arrangements.

The reasons higher levels of interrelatedness require harmonization or standardization are fairly straightforward and are twofold. First, some *regulatory* rules of the road are needed to prevent inconsistent actions from nullifying or diminishing the effectiveness of policies pursued by any one government. For example, if two or more governments pursue widely different interest-rate policies in governing money supplies, short-term capital could move away from the society where prevailing interest rates are low, thus reducing rather than enlarging the money supply, and toward the one where prevailing rates are high, thus enlarging rather than reducing the money supply. Second, harmonization and standardization are desirable as means of assuring an adequate *distribution* of benefits among a set of countries. They enhance the likelihood that all will benefit—or suffer—on a relatively equitable basis by preventing distortions to the flow of capital, goods, and services.

A higher level of interdependence among advanced industrial societies—not yet reached today and not likely to be attained during the coming decade—will involve efforts of a redistributive nature, with some governments actually transferring income to others. This will likely be required because of structural rather than cyclical problems that will develop for some societies as their economies become more highly integrated with others. If, as a result of the general level of economic integration, the industrial structures of some societies suffer unduly, their governments may well find the costs of international market integration too great. This can happen if, for example, a society's industry becomes uncompetitive in key sectors upon which much past economic growth was based—steel or shipbuilding or textiles— and if structural unemployment requires new capital investment the society itself cannot generate. To preserve economic integration in this situation, some redistribution of income would clearly be needed.

A high level of economic interdependence, in short, could well create the need for a jointly financed regional policy within the industrial world. In order to keep the group of countries together, politics in the area will involve what some scholars have recently termed the "collective elaboration of welfare choices." Since redistribution is likely to be virtually impossible in an international system composed of sovereign states, the only practical way to accomplish redistributive ends will be complex bargaining across a number of trade, monetary, macroeconomic, and even defense policy issues. Indeed, aspects of this sort of "linkage" politics have existed to some degree even with respect to macroeconomic issues. But there has been only a glimmering. It is not likely that levels of interdependence in the industrial world will be so high during the next decade that the need for coordinating policy on fundamental structural questions will arise generally. But the tight economic interdependence within the European Community might well make this level of coordination desirable among EC members.

CREATING COLLECTIVE LEADERSHIP

Typologies about coordinating policies may be useful analytically, but they do not serve as policy guidelines about how a process of collective management could be set in train. As we argued earlier, much will depend on the experience gained through experimentation in the coming years. But beyond the need for pragmatism in confronting issues as they arise there are also a number of more specific steps that governments could take.

Cooperation in general, especially collective leadership, will be feasible for governments if and only if they perceive that through it they will be better able to deal with domestic problems or gain support from certain interest groups and minimize opposition from others. This motivation behind cooperation can be seen in the first economic summit, held in France in the fall of 1975. Both the German and French governments, but especially the Germans, wanted to use the meeting to bolster sagging domestic support by demonstrating that their economic problems could be handled only by joint action with the United States. Yet both governments also were in a no-lose situation in that they could blame the American government for what they might have considered to be inappropriate policies or an unwillingness to cooperate. Had the United States government agreed to adopt expansionary policies to help them induce export-led growth, they could have pointed to their success in pressuring the United States. If the American government had failed to adopt policies that they considered desirable, they could have blamed the failure of their economic recovery programs on President Ford. Clearly, substantial political benefits to governments in their national political arenas are a vital precondition for even the most primitive attempts at collective leadership.

Ironically—and somewhat in opposition to the need to satisfy domestic interests—the other basic prerequisite to the establishment of collective leadership is the need to develop a more cosmopolitan attitude on the part of all the major industrial countries. Cosmopolitanism in this context entails two shifts in the orientation that governments should be taking toward one another in their strategies for demand management. First is the need to orient domestic policies within a more general framework that places an emphasis on the collective well-being of the industrial societies and, even more broadly, of the world economy. In short, an overall vision of collective welfare should become a higher priority than it has been in the past, and policies concerning national welfare should be developed within that general framework.

Second, governments need to recognize that their own domestic policies are of *legitimate* concern to their major economic partners and these partners have a right to influence those policies. There appears to be a growing awareness of this need among Europeans. For some years the European governments, especially the French, were reluctant to join with the United States in any regularized series of meetings at a deeper level than those of the OECD. They viewed this type of institutionalization as a vehicle of United States domination, which could impede European economic integration. However, it now seems that many governments desire to create a forum in which they can have a voice in influencing the course of American domestic economic policies. They have discovered that they cannot foster European economic integration without also taking into account the direction of domestic and foreign economic policy in the United States.

Politics—especially constituency and electoral politics—is the major impediment to the development of the necessary cosmopolitanism. In one sense, this impediment is a proper one. The welfare of national citizens ought to be the major concern of each government and, as a practical matter, electoral politics will continue to make this the case. But a number of organizational structures within governments can help to increase the political sensitivity each government requires to the domestic concerns of others. The exact formula for doing this varies from country

17

to country. In what follows we discuss how this applies to the United States.

The beginnings of an American policy that takes into account the interests of the other large economies requires organizational and attitudinal changes within the United States government. What has to be avoided and overcome is the tendency within the American government to compartmentalize issues according to "functions," such as Most Favored Nation (MFN) trade policy, nuclear proliferation policy, exchange-rate policy, NATO policy, etc. A more integrated approach is required which allows—indeed forces—public officials to assess the impact of a range of issues in American policy on individual economic partners. Within this framework a variety of American objectives can be judged according to how major economic partners are affected. Otherwise the government will frustrate key economies such as Germany and Japan, who would under the best circumstances see in United States policy an uncoordinated, unconcerted series of disjointed strands and would under worse conditions perceive a more malign and manipulative American approach.

An example of the type of policy that could be avoided is found in perceptions within the German government of American policy toward the Federal Republic in the early years of the Carter administration. American efforts in different functional areas affected Germany adversely. Efforts to induce the Germans to accelerate growth so as to act as an economic "locomotive" for Europe were regarded as insensitive to the German preference for maintaining price stability. American attacks on German-Brazilian nuclear cooperation in the name of an antiproliferation policy were seen as attempts to decrease German exports of nuclear energy plants. Defense procurement policies in the United States regarding a new generation of tanks were felt to represent a reversal of an American commitment to the Federal Republic on joint procurement of some German-manufactured equipment. And Carter's rhetoric about the development and deployment of a neutron bomb left a more committed German government embarrassed in confronting domestic opposition groups.

While a more coherent and balanced internal organizational structure within the American government, which took into account Germany's interests on a variety of issues, would not necessarily prevent conflicts over particular issues, it could go a long way toward minimizing those conflicts in setting a framework for cooperation. In essence this amounts to an emphasis on a "country desk" approach, which brings all the issues that concern a specific country together in order to make priorities and coordinate decisions. This arrangement, of course, runs the risk of frustrating functional continuity in policy making and creating gross inconsistencies in how different nations are treated. What is called for, then, is a delicate balance of these two points of view rather than an excessive emphasis on one or the other.

Beyond the organizational issue is the more general matter of the United States leadership role in the world economy. The essays by Gordon and Pelkmans present two different faces of this role and reflect the national perspectives of the two authors. Gordon argues that the major concern of demand management in the United States should be *domestic* conditions. Demand management should aim at price stability and full employment to the degree that the two do not conflict. For Gordon, the most sensible *international* role for the United States is to make sure that its own house is in order. Pelkmans' attitude toward the United States reflects a more generalized European fear that the domestic and international objectives of American economic policy are as likely as not going to conflict with one another, and when this happens, domestic objectives will predominate.

These potential conflicts between American domestic and international concerns are obvious. For example, if the quest for full employment at home is pursued by loosening the reins on the money supply this could result in short-term capital flows abroad, inducing inflation in Europe. Furthermore, this type of expansionary monetary policy, or even the investment-oriented fiscal stimulus proposed by Gordon, would increase US imports and could—in the absence of policy coordination among OECD members—cause a deterioration in the US balance of trade. This could lead to a depreciation of the dollar, which would disrupt economic security in Europe and put pressure on OPEC to raise oil prices. This stimulus to the U.S. economy might also encourage the Japanese to rely on the U.S. market rather than taking steps to cut back their exports by accepting a higher level of domestic unemployment. In short, if U.S. demand management policies are not coordinated within the OECD, their effects could be harmful, even when they are aimed at economic expansion.

The economic and political factors contributing to this ambivalent position of the United States as a kind of awkward big brother all point to one similar aspect of the future American role. The United States is involved in an increasingly symmetrical form of economic interdependence with its Western partners. This was not always the case. During the period of U.S. predominance, the American economy was large enough and closed enough not to be politically disrupted by foreign economic disturbances. The decline in size relative to the Europeans and Japanese and greater economic openness add to American sensitivity and vulnerability to international economic events. In addition, the significance of the U.S. dollar in international monetary affairs and the importance of United States agricultural exports also add to interdependence. Finally, the economic summits and discussions between leaders of the advanced industrial states emphasize their mutual dependence.

This growing United States sensitivity to the process of economic integration seems likely to increase in the next decade. The feeling of vulnerability that accompanies economic interdependence gives the United States interests in both preserving its domestic position and sustaining the existing system of international economic relations. A tension thus results between an inward-looking and an outward-looking stance. At the extremes, the United States in the 1980s can either stress its own domestic interests exclusively or be as concerned with system maintenance as it was during the cold war. There are clearly several options that lie between these two poles. It is important to note that economic interdependence can potentially provide a basis for a persuasive and cooperative United States attitude in its relations with the other key Western economies. Rather than being based on the hegemony of the past, the United States leadership role could be based on the growing similarity of its interests and concerns with those of the Europeans and the Japanese.

In practical terms this kind of American leadership—based on the identity of interests among advanced industrial states—encourages all these nations to face common problems, such as the distribution of deficits arising from OECD-area oil imports, in a cooperative manner. In the context of the sluggish economic recovery of the late 1970s, this means, for example, that it is incumbent upon the United States to produce an effective energy policy if it expects the Germans and Japanese to stimulate their domestic economies and reduce their inherent trade surpluses. Providing a cooperative example through its actions is a complex challenge to American politicians and bureaucrats. In the 1980s the convergence of OECD interests, combined with the size and strength of the United States economy, makes this kind of American leadership role possible; but failure to achieve consensus among the key Western governments could also encourage the United States to protect itself from outside interference by substantially cutting itself off from its economic partners.

Whether collective leadership can be developed to supplant, or at least to supplement, American predominance depends as much upon the attitudes of the governments of Japan, Germany, France, and some of the other advanced industrial countries as it does on the United States, but the United States remains the pivotal figure. Although it has declined in relative economic importance, it still remains by far the largest individual economy in the world, with the most generalized impact as the largest trading nation and with the dollar continuing to be the most significant transaction and reserve currency. Nevertheless its position in the world economy cannot guarantee that American policy objectives will automatically be achieved. Its enduring economic significance does, however, mean that no generalized cooperation on policy will occur or be successful without an American policy that takes into account the interests of the other large economies, including those of Japan, Germany, France, the United Kingdom, and Italy.

Beyond what the United States does unilaterally, cooperation obviously will also require international compromises and agreements among the wider arena of governments. Here we must draw a distinction between *who* should be involved and *what form* of politics would be most constructive in creating a framework for collective leadership. Both issues are difficult to resolve and will require more experimentation and experience.

At times the governments involved are likely to include only those of the three largest economies—the United States, Japan, and the Federal Republic—while at other times France, the United Kingdom, Saudi Arabia, Italy, and Canada will also be involved. While it now seems to be the case that consultations among the governments of the United States, Japan, Britain, France, and West Germany can more efficiently resolve differences over the management of common problems than can any other grouping of governments, it is not necessarily the case that the same grouping will be the right one for problems that arise 3, 5, or 10 years from now. For this reason it is best to wait until a more appropriate time to make decisions about which governments should be the principal participants in formally institutionalized policy coordination.

Whoever is involved, it is clear that one of the central forms of politics among them will be based on linkages. It has often been observed that the linkage of so many countries and policy instruments to each other has led to paralysis in the international economy. Policy action, domestically or internationally, can readily be neutralized by its own effects or by the actions of others. Yet linkage can also serve as a basis for international agreement. This is especially the case when different governments seek different goals, since it is often easier for them to trade off their preferences through international cooperation. Germany's preference for lower inflation and higher unemployment might well be traded against the French preference for lower unemployment and higher inflation in working out agreements. Having noted this about linkages, it is doubtful that any other general points can be made about the useful time to link or to delink policies and programs to facilitate international cooperation.

It is clear, however, that in the future linkage politics will be

22

more effective if the general state of the international conjuncture is favorable. Policy coordination is likely to be most successful in periods when economic diversity is great and domestic economic cycles are out of phase. It is also more successful or at least more feasible in periods of sustained economic growth, such as that characterized by the 1960s as a whole. It is extremely difficult to achieve when the economies are in phase and in recession simultaneously, because no country is then in a position to induce growth elsewhere by increasing its imports from the others.

As a result of the impact of the new economic nationalism, there is great pressure among the major economic powers of the West for an institutionalization of consultations on demand management policies. Regular meetings can have significance even when they are not productive, because they are symbolically meaningful. Furthermore, there is also the possibility that regular talks will eventually produce real progress in policy cooperation.

As noted above, the 1980s appear at best to be a time for exploration and experimentation with the process of developing collective leadership for the economies of the key Western industrial countries. The essays in this volume should be seen as one step in this process of experimentation; they advance the ongoing dialogue on the international management of macroeconomic policies.

Domestic Macroeconomic Policy: A Review, Preview, and Prescription

Robert J. Gordon

ONE

Policy Activism and the Surprises of the Past Decade

The public may be excused if it approaches with some skepticism any attempt by an economist to peer into the macroeconomic future. Journalists have convinced their readers that macroeconomics has been stood on its head: in place of the mid-1960s' policy trade-off, which offered the chance to achieve lower unemployment at the cost of only modestly higher inflation, the 1970s have witnessed a doubling of *both* unemployment and inflation rates of the 1960s.[1] Forecasts by economists will not

[1]These figures are for the United States; some countries have fared worse. Comparing the latest available 1976 monthly unemployment rate and the first-half of 1976 annual rate of inflation with the average for 1960–1969, we find that the recent figure is the following percentage of the earlier figure, for each of the main industrial countries:

	Unemployment	Inflation
Britain	340%	290%
France	300	235
Germany	520	120
Italy	110	540
Japan	170	90
U.S.	170	225

SOURCE: "The Traps Facing the U.S. Abroad," *Business Week*, November 15, 1976, p. 143.

be taken seriously unless the economists can convince both policy makers and the public that their recent failures represent a brief flare-up of the "forecasting flu" rather than symptoms of a terminal scientific illness.

THE CLASH BETWEEN MONETARIST RULES AND NONMONETARIST ACTIVISM

Not only has the public been disillusioned by the lack of advance warning of growing economic discomfort, but also it has been made wary by continuing disagreements among economists. Can economics be considered a science any longer if its most famous practitioners consistently divide into two camps that offer conflicting policy advice? Worse yet, can the coincidence between the divergent policy recommendations and political allegiances of the two camps be entirely ignored?

Usage has centered on the term *monetarism* (less often *the Chicago School* or *Friedmanites* or just *conservatives*) to describe the school of thought that supports regulating the supply of money according to a rule specifying a constant monetary growth rate. Among the many issues on which economists cannot agree is a label for the school of thought that opposes the monetarists. Since monetarists have appeared to claim that only money is important, while their opponents have always treated *both* monetary and fiscal changes as basic determinants of income, *fiscalist* is an entirely inaccurate label for the opponents. Similarly, the labels *Keynesian* or *neo-Keynesian* connote wage rigidity (an assumption used in Keynes's classic treatise) and are inappropriate because no serious *monetarist opponent* assumes that wages are fixed, at least in analyses in which that assumption matters.[2] The label *eclectics* is most accurate but also most insulting in a world in which eclectics are often considered soft-

---

[2] The best evidence of concern with the flexibility of wages is contained in the large number of studies of wage determination conducted by or sponsored by the opponents of the monetarists. A representative collection is in Otto Eckstein (ed.), *The Econometrics of Price Determination: Conference*, Federal Reserve, Washington, D.C., 1972.

headed. So perhaps the label *nonmonetarist* is least offensive and in fact appears to have caught on, although it still carries the completely inaccurate connotation that the monetarists' opponents believe money does not matter.

The great irony of the debate between monetarists and nonmonetarists is that the impact of money on unemployment and inflation is not the central issue! For the past 15 years attention has been diverted by a small band of economists at Yale and MIT who have claimed that the dispute pits a monetarist view that "only money matters" with a nonmonetarist view that "both monetary and fiscal policy matter." For instance, James Tobin of Yale University has repeatedly claimed that the main issue is the empirical validity of a particular theoretical condition required for fiscal policy to influence real output in the short run. Yet as early as 1966 the chief monetarist, Milton Friedman, admitted in writing that fiscal policy could affect real output in the short run and the price level in the long run.[3] So the nonmonetarists deserve blame for continuing an irrelevant debate long after it was settled.

Instead, the real dispute between monetarists and nonmonetarists has nothing to do with the relative potency of monetary versus fiscal policy. The central clash revolves around the location in the economy of the principal source of instability. Monetarists believe the private economy is basically stable, that ill-conceived and poorly timed government actions cause economic instability. Nonmonetarists pinpoint private spending decisions as the main source of instability and generally support an "activist" government countercyclical policy (both monetary and fiscal) to achieve economic stability.

To add one irony to another, both the monetarist and nonmonetarist camps regard the decade of the Great Depression as

---

[3]A volume containing the papers essential for an introduction to the main elements of the debate of the past decade is Robert J. Gordon (ed.), *Milton Friedman's Monetary Framework*, University of Chicago Press, Chicago, 1974. A short summary is available in Robert J. Gordon, "Comments on Modigliani and Ando," in Jerome Stein (ed.), *Monetarism*, North-Holland Publishing Co., Amsterdam, 1976, pp. 52–66. Other afterthoughts on the debate are contained in the comments by Fischer, Friedman, and Tobin in the Stein volume.

providing the most dramatic example of instability originating from, respectively, the government and the private sector. Monetarists point to the contribution to the severity of the Depression of the 31 percent 1929–1933 decline in the money supply, whereas nonmonetarists emphasize the 85 percent decline in private investment during the same interval and add that even in the years 1936–1939, when the money supply had substantially surpassed its 1929 level, private investment was on average still 40 percent below that of 1929.

A "monetarist platform," of my own design, helps to clarify the issues that are still subjects of lively debate. The four planks of the platform are:

1. Without the interference of "demand shocks" introduced by erratic government policy, private spending would be stable, primarily because consumption is the largest component of private spending and varies with households' slowly adjusting concept of their long-run or "permanent" income.[4]
2. Even if private planned spending is not completely stable, flexible prices create a natural tendency for it to come back on course.[5]
3. Even if private planned spending is not completely stable and prices are not completely flexible, an activist monetary and fiscal policy to counteract private-demand swings is likely to do more harm than good.
4. Even if prices are not completely flexible, so that the economy can wander away from the best attainable unemployment rate in the short run, there can be no dispute regarding the increased flexibility of prices the longer the period of time allowed for adjustment.

Virtually every dispute about economic policy during the 1970s

[4]Milton Friedman, *A Theory of the Consumption Function*, Princeton University Press, Princeton, 1957.

[5]The best introduction to the capabilities and limitations of flexible prices as a self-correcting mechanism is James Tobin, "Keynesian Models of Recession and Depression," *American Economic Review*, vol. 65, May 1975, pp. 195–202.

can be interpreted as a disagreement between monetarists and nonmonetarists over the validity of planks 2 and 4 in the monetarist platform. During the 1970–1971 and 1975–1976 periods of relatively high unemployment, monetarists recommended much slower rates of monetary growth than did nonmonetarists, both because they believed that any temporary unemployment caused by slow demand growth would be eliminated by a rapid decline in the rate of inflation (plank 2) and because they did not care much about short-run changes in unemployment. With their long-term time horizon, their gaze leapt over any transient extra unemployment to concentrate on the lower rate of inflation that would result in future decades (plank 4).[6]

In some recession situations of high unemployment, as occurred in 1975 in the United States, the monetarist distaste for activist policy would appear to condemn the economy to a longer recession than would the alternative nonmonetarist approach of monetary or fiscal stimulation. Yet monetarists deny that their recommendation reflects a choice between more or less unemployment now, saying that it is only a choice between a lesser reduction in unemployment now and a greater increase in unemployment later. Why? Because they distrust the political process, which is said to throw up great obstacles to achievement of sensible economic policy. The economy is bound to overshoot any target, they would argue, and politicians are unlikely to have the courage to apply the brakes to the economy soon enough to allow a "soft landing" at the target unemployment rate. Instead the economy will be allowed to expand too far and too rapidly, inflation will accelerate, and the Federal Reserve will be forced to cause another recession and bout of unemployment in order to fight the renewed acceleration of inflation.

[6]Specific examples and a more extended discussion are in Gordon, "Comments on Modigliani and Ando," pp. 55–58. The classic monetarist attempt to reinterpret the importance of an increase in unemployment is Milton Friedman, "Unemployment Figures," *Newsweek*, October 20, 1969, reprinted in his *An Economist's Protest, Second Edition*, Thomas Horton, Glen Ridge, 1975, pp. 105–107. An extended answer to Friedman's column is Robert J. Gordon, "The Welfare Cost of Higher Unemployment," *Brookings Papers on Economic Activity*, vol. 4, no. 1, 1973, pp. 133–95.

In the end the basic conflicts in policy recommendations by economists do not originate in irreconcilable analytical differences that call into question the scientific claims of economics. The dispute over planks 1 and 3 is a matter not of right or wrong but of differences in emphasis, perhaps the most important of which is the greater nonmonetarist willingness to trust the government to follow the advice of economists, as contrasted with the fundamental distrust of the political process exhibited by monetarists. Plank 2, on the flexibility of prices, remains in dispute because the historical data do not send strong signals that would allow economists to predict the speed of adjustment of inflation to higher unemployment. Finally, the disagreement over plank 4, on the importance of the short run as opposed to the long run, reflects not only differing value judgments but also differing degrees of optimism regarding the payoff of short-run policy shifts.[7]

WHOSE CASE HAS BEEN STRENGTHENED BY THE EVENTS OF THE PAST DECADE?

The intellectual tide during the past decade shifted first, in the late 1960s, toward the monetarist position that policy activism does more harm than good but then, in the 1970s, has begun to ebb back toward support of the nonmonetarist case for activism. There is no question that the most profound development limiting the potential scope of activism in the decade was the acceptance by the profession of the "natural-rate hypothesis." In the mid-1960s policy choices had been framed in terms of the trade-off between unemployment and inflation. A lower unemployment rate could be achieved and maintained permanently by stimulative monetary and fiscal policies, at the cost of a permanently higher but stable rate of inflation. It had been common in the United States for economic advisers to Democratic presidents

[7]This interpretation of the monetarist debate is partly based on discussions and correspondence with Milton Friedman in the spring of 1977. A more complete treatment is contained in Robert J. Gordon, *Macroeconomics*, Little, Brown, Boston, 1978, chap. 12.

to recommend both a lower unemployment rate and higher inflation rate than the target of Republican advisers.

Milton Friedman was the first to state explicitly that "there is no long-run stable trade-off between inflation and unemployment" and to formulate the natural-rate hypothesis that any attempt by policy makers to hold unemployment permanently below the natural rate of unemployment would cause inflation to accelerate continuously. Although the old-fashioned mid-1960s trade-off view had correctly been that a reduction in unemployment would raise the inflation rate above the rate generally expected by the public, the subsequent upward revision of expectations and the resulting further upward push on the inflation rate had been neglected.

The natural-rate hypothesis drastically limited the possibilities for control of the unemployment rate through monetary and fiscal activism. No longer could an administration choose its own favorite point on a stable unemployment-inflation trade-off curve. A permanent reduction in actual unemployment could be achieved without accelerating inflation only through microeconomic policies operating directly on the natural unemployment rate—for instance, government labor programs, subsidies to bribe firms to train workers, and reductions in the minimum wage and in other barriers to the flexibility of wages. In the long run monetary policy could affect only the rate of inflation, and fiscal policy, while having a minor impact on the price level, was not a stabilization tool but rather an allocative instrument responsible for determining the proportions of total output consisting of consumption, investment, and government spending.

The natural rate hypothesis, while drastically changing the long-run analysis of macroeconomic policy, still left a role for monetary and fiscal activism in the short run. If an unexpected decline in business or consumer spending were to cause an increase in actual unemployment above the natural rate, a monetary or fiscal stimulus could still act to shorten the recession and return actual unemployment more rapidly to the natural rate than would occur without policy intervention. But in the late 1960s economists began to reconsider the merits of short-run fiscal "fine tuning."

33

The "new economics" of Walter Heller and the other members of the Kennedy-Johnson Council of Economic Advisers had emphasized changes in personal income tax rates as the most efficient means of achieving short-run stabilization. Monetary policy was less efficient because of long lags between accelerations of money and subsequent responses of spending; increases in government spending of any substantial magnitude were likely to be squandered on ill-conceived projects unless a substantial delay was allowed for careful program design; and, in the tax area, the United States government was forced to concentrate on the personal income tax in the absence of any substantial broad-based federal sales or value-added tax. While plank 1 of the monetarists' platform allows a *permanent* income tax cut immediately to stimulate consumption spending as households raise their estimate of permanent income, no such strong stimulus can be exerted by a *temporary* tax change that is generally expected to be reversed in a year or two.[8] And, by its very nature, short-run fiscal fine tuning designed to offset *temporary* fluctuations in private spending desires must rely on *temporary* tax rate changes.

Fiscal fine tuners are still left with excise-type taxes as a potential tool. Unfortunately for stabilization purposes, the fiscal authority in the United States is divided between the administration and Congress, and long delays between the initiation and final passage of tax change proposals have been common. Legislative delays cause changes in sales and excise taxes, including the investment tax credit, to work perversely. For instance, a proposal to suspend the investment tax credit in order to dampen the economy in an economic boom will, during congressional debate on the proposal, cause firms to accelerate projects that allow them to qualify for the credit and create a destabilizing burst of *extra* investment spending.

The case for policy activism would be strengthened if economists had consistently accumulated an accurate record of fore-

[8]Oddly enough this point was first popularized by a nonmonetarist. See Robert Eisner, "Fiscal and Monetary Policy Reconsidered," *American Economic Review*, vol. 59, December 1969, pp. 897–905.

casting cyclical turning points in advance. With enough advance notice monetary and fiscal changes could have their desired impact when needed, despite the time lags (primarily an "effectiveness lag" for monetary policy and a "legislative lag" for fiscal policy). Unfortunately forecasters have missed enough important events of the past decade, particularly the continuing acceleration of inflation in 1968–1969 and the inflation–cum–severe recession in 1974–1975, to make accurate forecasting a weak reed upon which to lean the case for policy activism.

The arsenal of tools for macroeconomic activism includes not only monetary and fiscal policy but also wage and price controls. The final nail in the coffin of the case for activism, from the point of view of monetarists, is the failure of the United States control program of 1971–1974. While the price level (measured by the deflator for private nonfarm output) was held down by as much as 3 to 4 percent in 1972 and 1973, there was a price rebound of about the same magnitude in 1974, after the controls were lifted. The controls made no contribution at all to lowering the long-run rate of inflation, and they actually destabilized real output and unemployment by adding to consumer real incomes during the overheated 1972 business expansion and subtracting from real incomes during the last half of 1974.

As their remedy for the limitations of activism, monetarists have a simple prescription: expand the money supply at a constant rate, i.e., follow a "constant growth-rate rule." The only excuse for any variation in the constant growth-rate rule occurs if inflation is proceeding at a rate higher than is desirable in the long run, in which case the steady monetary growth rate should be gradually reduced. If unemployment happens to be above the natural unemployment rate, there is no need to accelerate monetary growth, since the required stimulus to real incomes can come from a steady reduction in the rate of inflation.

During most of the 1960s nonmonetarists ignored the constant growth-rate rule in the belief that the successful use of fiscal stimulation between 1962 and 1965 to lower the unemployment rate created a prima facie case for activism. As the limitations of activism became evident in the late 1960s, however, some economists turned to systematic empirical retrospective com-

35

parisons of the constant growth-rate rule with alternative mechanical formulas that allow monetary growth to respond to changes in unemployment and inflation. The best of this work consists of a series of papers by J. Phillip Cooper and Stanley Fischer, demonstrating with several different econometric models that a constant growth-rate rule would have been destabilizing relative to more flexible formulas during the 1950s and 1960s.[9]

Monetarists have not been convinced by these tests, both because they have no faith in the underlying econometric models of the economy, and because they believe that the structure of the economy would not have remained invariant to the particular policies pursued (whereas the use of an econometric model for retrospective policy comparisons holds the structure of the economy constant).[10] So nonmonetarists have turned to other lines of argument, primarily an attack on planks 1 and 2 of the monetarist platform. In a nutshell, they claim, the 1970s have produced new evidence that denies *both* that private current-dollar spending is stable *and* that the price level adjusts with reasonable speed to insulate real output from shifts in current-dollar demand.

The essence of the nonmonetarist case rests on the undeniable fact that the almost unprecedented instability of unemployment and prices during the 1970s occurred despite the adherence by the Federal Reserve to a policy quite close to a constant growth-rate rule. Between December 1969 and December 1977 the average growth rate of "M2" (currency and deposits at commercial banks) was 9.8 percent per year and the maximum deviation from the average in any one year was only 1.5 percent.[11] Despite this record of stable monetary growth, the economy suffered from an unstable unemployment rate (ranging from 4.6 percent in late

[9]The basic theoretical issues and references to the empirical tests can be found in Stanley Fischer and J. Phillip Cooper, "Stabilization Policy and Lags," *Journal of Political Economy*, vol. 81, July/August 1973, pp. 847–877.

[10]The basic statement of the "endogenous structure" argument is Robert E. Lucas, Jr., "Econometric Policy Evaluation: A Critique," *Journal of Monetary Economics*, vol. 2, supplement to January 1976 issue, pp. 19–46.

[11]The story for M1 (excluding commercial bank time deposits) is almost the same: an average growth rate of 6.1 percent and a maximum deviation of only 1.7 percent with the single exception of the 2.8 percent deviation in 1972. All figures refer to growth rates over 12-month intervals between December and December.

1973 to 8.9 percent in May 1975) and from a wildly gyrating inflation rate (ranging from only 3 percent in early 1972 to over 13 percent in late 1974).

Part of the instability of both unemployment and inflation during this period was caused by the implementation and termination of wage and price controls and should obviously not be included in the case against the monetarists who uniformly opposed the control program. Nonetheless the nonmonetarist case for activism was strengthened by four separate features of economic events in the 1970s which cast doubt on the ability of the private economy to achieve self-governing stable growth without government intervention (this list might be called the "nonmonetarist manifesto").

1. Since the 1930s the instability of private investment, as formalized in the theory of the investment "accelerator," has been the centerpiece of the case for government stabilization policy. A broader view recognizes that consumer durables also are subject to large fluctuations. In the 1970s the share of durable goods output in GNP continued its marked gyrations, surging from 16.5 percent in 1971 to 19.0 percent in 1973, in line with the range of variation that had caused economic instability in the 1950s (especially the decline from 17.9 percent in 1955 to 14.9 percent in 1958) and in the 1960s (a range from 14.9 percent in 1961 to 18.1 percent in 1966).

2. The case for the constant growth-rate rule monetary policy is absolutely dependent on the stability and predictability of the real demand for money relative to real income and interest rates. But since 1974 all previous money-demand equations used for forecasting have fallen apart as the result of the mysteriously low growth of money. If the economy had been at its natural rate of unemployment and desired long-run inflation target during this period, then the unexpected shortfall of money demand would have caused a constant growth-rate rule policy to overstimulate the economy.[12]

[12]When the demand for money is subject to unexpected shocks, a case can be made for a monetary policy that attempts to stabilize the interest rate rather than the money supply. See William Poole, "Optimal Choice of Monetary Policy Instruments in a Simple Stochastic Macro Model," *Quarterly Journal of Economics*, vol. 84, May 1970, pp. 197–216.

3. The single most important novelty of the 1970s has been the advent of the "supply shock," which has had a profound impact on the analytical framework of macroeconomic policy. An increase in the price of oil or a crop failure causes simultaneously a direct reduction of real income as society's productive capability is diminished, together with a higher price level as the higher costs of oil or food are passed on in the form of higher prices for final goods. If the monetary authority adheres to a constant growth-rate rule, there is no additional money available to finance the higher value of transactions, and as a consequence a secondary indirect reduction in economywide real output is required to bring the demand for money into line with the fixed supply.[13] The food and oil supply shocks together wih the one-shot increase in the price level in 1974 following the termination of United States price controls were the essential causes of the severe worldwide inflationary recession of 1974–1975.

4. Neither investment instability, money-demand surprises, nor supply shocks would cause output instability if wages and prices were perfectly and instantaneously flexible. In such a world a reduction in the demand for goods or an increase in the demand for money would cause an immediate drop in the price level without any extra unemployment. A supply shock, for instance, a crop failure, would be followed immediately by a reduction in the price of nonfarm products sufficient to maintain full employment in the nonfarm sector, thus eliminating the indirect secondary-output "multiplier effect" of supply shocks. *It is the sluggish downward adjustment of prices in response to high unemployment, caused fundamentally by the long-term nature of labor contracts, which prevents the private economy from maintaining stable output growth in the face of demand and supply shocks.*

The 1970s added new evidence on the stickiness of wages. There was no decline in the rate of wage growth during the 1970–1971 recession. The 8.7 percent annual rate of wage growth

[13]A simple theoretical analysis of the macroeconomic multiplier effect of supply shocks is contained in Robert J. Gordon, "Alternative Responses of Policy to External Supply Shocks," *Brookings Papers on Economic Activity*, vol. 6, no. 1, 1975, pp. 183–206.

recorded in the first three quarters of 1977 was actually faster than the 7.7 percent average of the preceding six years, despite unprecedented levels of unemployment in 1975 and 1976.[14] In the face of a constant growth-rate rule monetary policy, the private economy can attain the natural rate of unemployment only if the rate of wage growth decelerates markedly, and so far the required wage deceleration has occurred at a snail's pace. In current macroeconomic policy debates the crucial role of long-term labor contracts, which inhibit the economy's ability to correct output fluctuations without government interference, brings us full circle to a revival of Keynesian economics based on the assumption of wage rigidity that plays so large a role in Keynes' *General Theory*.

NEW POLICY TOOLS

Given the limitations of simple policy remedies, both the monetarist constant growth-rate rule and the nonmonetarist fine-tuned temporary tax cuts, it is not surprising that alternative policy tools have received increasing emphasis. Monetarists and nonmonetarists alike have embraced the escalation, or *indexation*, of wage contracts, financial assets, and tax brackets, although for differing reasons.

Nonmonetarist James Tobin endorses the issuance by the federal government of long-term bonds that guarantee a fixed real rate of return (and therefore pay a nominal rate of return equal to the guarantee plus the rate of inflation). Tobin, perhaps the most forceful opponent of the government policies of 1970–1971 and 1974–1976 which deliberately created unemployment to fight inflation, finds indexation attractive because it reduces the damage done by inflation to asset holders and thus lessens the pressure on the government to pursue anti-inflationary policies.

Monetarist Milton Friedman supports indexation because it prevents the government from imposing "taxation without representation." Indexed bonds protect the savers who finance gov-

---

[14]*Wage growth* refers to average hourly compensation for all employees in the nonfarm business sector.

ernment deficits, particularly during wartime, and who in the past have been expropriated by postwar inflation. Indexation of tax brackets prevents inflation from pushing individual taxpayers into higher tax brackets, and thus also prevents inflation from automatically raising the share of government tax revenue in national income.

If the economy were only subject to demand shocks, that is, fluctuations in the demand for commodities and money, indexation would be a boon to monetarists and nonmonetarists alike. Wage rates would no longer be fixed by long-term contracts but would be free to adjust much more rapidly in response to movements of the actual unemployment rate either above or below the natural rate. Unfortunately supply shocks dim the allure of indexation, just as they reduce the attractiveness of a monetary constant growth-rate rule. Wage indexation, which fixes real wages in advance, interferes with the adjustment of real wages required by a supply shock. Indexation aggravates both unemployment and inflation in the aftermath of a supply shock, and thus an optimal system would allow only partial indexation of wages.[15]

Since the natural-rate hypothesis deprived nonmonetarists of the possibility of reducing unemployment below the natural rate by applying stimulative monetary and fiscal policies, their attention has turned to consideration of government policies that would reduce the natural rate of unemployment itself. Thus one effect of the natural-rate hypothesis was to bring to the forefront a long menu of "microeconomic" or "structural" labor market policies, including reforms in the unemployment compensation system to reduce the incentive for extended job search, and a number of possible methods to improve the "matching" of job requirements with the locations and skills of job seekers, including an improved employment service to provide better in-

[15]The first to provide a formal analysis of wage indexation in the presence of supply shocks was Joanna Gray, "Wage Indexation: A Macroeconomic Approach," *Journal of Monetary Economics*, vol. 2, April 1976, pp. 221–36. A numerical simulation of the consequences of wage indexation in the presence of a crop failure is contained in Gordon, "Alternative Responses of Policy to External Supply Shocks," op. cit. in footnote 13.

formation on job vacancies and training subsidies to private firms or government-sponsored training of workers. In this area the only dispute between the two groups is ideological, with the monetarists favoring changes that reduce governmental interference with the private sector (eliminating or reforming unemployment compensation and the minimum wage) and with the nonmonetarists recommending new government programs to enable disadvantaged individuals to qualify for available job openings.

Nonmonetarists also part company with monetarists in their imaginative suggestions for new tax plans to deal with inflationary recessions and destabilizing supply shocks. Relatively traditional schemes would deal with agricultural price fluctuations due to crop failures by using a buffer-stock reserve or a tax subsidy plan ("fiscal stabilization fund") to offset farm-price movements. The monopoly rents earned by the Organization of Petroleum Exporting Countries (OPEC) can be reduced by means of an import tax on oil. Such a tax raises the price of oil above the OPEC level and thus reduces the net flow of revenues from the industrialized countries to OPEC and provides funds for fiscal subsidies in the industrialized countries to mitigate the macroeconomic multiplier effects of oil-price increases.[16]

Nonmonetarists also are willing to attempt to tilt the short-run inflation-unemployment trade-off curve by using fiscal incentives. In general, a tax cut reduces the inflationary impact of a given increase in real output by reducing the "tax wedge" between market prices and after-tax factor incomes, thus allowing workers to obtain a given increase in take-home pay with a smaller required increase in market prices. Some nonmonetarists are interested in using the tax system to enforce wage controls or "guidelines." Negotiated wage agreements above a specified threshold would be taxed away, and in some schemes below-average wage increases would be encouraged through the promise of a tax reduction.

Microeconomic allocative fiscal proposals include plans to deal

[16]Hendrik S. Houthakker, *The World Price of Oil*, American Enterprise Institute, Washington, D.C., 1976.

with the growing imbalance between labor input and primary materials production capacity: the transition to the natural rate of unemployment, roughly 5.5 percent, would be facilitated by a government stockpile plan that in high-unemployment years would buy steel, aluminum, and other materials subject to capacity shortages, so that the materials would be available to fuel the economy during high-output years. The need for the stockpile might disappear if several years of stable output growth at the natural unemployment rate induced private firms to build needed capacity.

EFFECTS OF FLOATING EXCHANGE RATES

The theory of domestic macroeconomic policy exists in a vacuum isolated from events in the rest of the world, thanks to the predominant influence in current economic thinking of economists from the very large United States economy, which for most purposes—with the obvious exception of oil prices—can be treated as closed. Until 1971 the Bretton Woods fixed-exchange-rate system allowed the United States an assymetric advantage because its currency was held as international reserves by other nations and its balance-of-payments deficits could be financed by the creation of additional dollar liabilities. The total world money supply resembled an inverted pyramid resting on a foundation consisting of the United States monetary base. Expansion of that base at a rate faster than desired in the rest of the world forced upon other nations the choice between inflation and revaluation, with the former solution chosen until 1971. Then, in the 1971–1973 interval, the old system broke down, exchange-rate adjustments occurred, and a new system of managed, floating exchange rates emerged.

In an ideal world with flexible commodity prices, floating exchange rates allow each nation autonomy in the achievement of its desired inflation target. As in a closed economy, NRH would require that an open economy use microeconomic labor-market policies to achieve permanent changes in unemployment. Unfortunately, the sluggish adjustment of prices to deviations of unemployment from the natural rate of unemployment further complicates macroeconomic policy in an open economy with floating exchange rates.

For a large economy such as the United States, with a small foreign sector, the complexities introduced by floating exchange rates are relatively minor. In a situation when unemployment is above the natural rate, as occurred in the United States in 1975 and 1976, policy makers face several alternative short-run inflation-unemployment trade-off curves depending on the particular type of stimulative policy chosen. A fiscal stimulus, achieved either through extra expenditures or a tax cut, raises the domestic demand for money and causes the dollar to appreciate, thus cutting the prices of traded goods and reducing the overall rate of inflation below that which a closed economy would experience in the same circumstances. The exchange appreciation also reduces the United States trade surplus (or increases the deficit) and cuts the output expansion yielded by a given fiscal stimulus, thus requiring a larger fiscal expansion to cut unemployment by a given amount.

Monetary policy under floating exchange rates in an open economy, on the other hand, has the reverse effects compared with a closed economy. A monetary stimulus that adds to the money supply causes the exchange rate to depreciate, adding to the prices of traded goods and raising the overall domestic rate of inflation. The depreciation also improves the trade surplus and thus cuts the amount of monetary stimulus required to achieve a given reduction in unemployment. From any given starting position above the natural rate of unemployment, then, policy makers face a relatively unfavorable "monetary expansion" short-run trade-off between inflation and unemployment, while the "fiscal expansion" trade-off is more favorable.

What policy autonomy does a small country possess if the large countries of the world are producing at levels below their "natural output" (i.e., the maximum output attainable without accelerating inflation), while their price levels are increasing as a result of built-in wage contracts negotiated in previous periods of excess demand? Maintenance of natural output by a small country in such an environment cannot occur at the initial exchange rate, since an increase in national output relative to the rest of the world will cause a trade deficit. In most small countries pure fiscal expansion without an accompanying increase in the money supply is difficult to achieve in the absence of an established market for domestic government bonds. Hence a monetary expansion and exchange depreciation are required to boost employment.

Time lags and foreign-exchange speculation may combine to defeat the aims of policy stimulation. First, the initial impact of an exchange depreciation is to raise the price of imports relative to exports for most countries, causing a deterioration in the terms of trade, a loss in domestic real income, and a dampening of domestic expenditure which may offset the policy stimulus. The increase in real demand for exports generated by the exchange depreciation takes time to occur, and in the meantime speculators may cause a further deterioration in the exchange rate. As a proposition in comparative statics, there should be some exchange rate that would allow a small country to achieve its employment target when the rest of the world is in a slump—if the long-run price elasticities of imports and exports are high enough—but the dynamic route to the employment and exchange-rate targets may be a long and unstable one.

TWO

A More General Theory of Inflation to Guide Predictions for the Next Decade

Just as the dispute between the monetarists and nonmonetarists originates in differences in both economic analysis and political values, so any prediction of the state of macroeconomic policy in the late 1980s requires a framework that combines economic and political elements. In this chapter we consider the sources of pressure for monetary accommodation placed on the central bank by both the private and government sectors, the political factors likely to control the response of the central bank, and then examine the reaction of wage- and price-setting agents in the private sector to the actions of the central bank.

THE DEMAND FOR MONETARY ACCOMMODATION

In the long run inflation must be fundamentally a monetary phenomenon. A 10 percent rate of monetary growth maintained over three decades would result in a rate of inflation roughly 10 percent higher than would be generated by a zero rate of monetary growth over the same period. But this mundane observation, accepted by monetarists and nonmonetarists alike, leaves open the underlying determinants of the long-run growth rate of money.

The classic source of pressure for monetary expansion comes from central-government deficits caused by wartime expenditures and postwar reconstruction. During the long period between the early 1600s and the early 1950s, every major inflation and hyperinflation in Europe and the United States was related to the needs of wartime or postwar government finance. Governments would depart from the gold standard when wars forced them to print their own money to finance deficits and would return to the gold standard as soon as possible after wars, for instance, in 1879 in the case of the United States after the Civil War and in 1925 in the case of the United Kingdom after World War I. Inflationary finance made sense as part of an optimal package of taxes in a wartime situation, since a mixture of conventional taxes and the "inflation tax" were likely to impose a smaller allocative burden than either category of taxation used alone.[17]

More controversial but probably more relevant for the 1980s is that a "cost push" by labor unions may be an additional source of pressure for monetary accommodation. If an economy is initially in a situation of equilibrium at the natural rate of unemployment, with wages increasing at the rate of expected inflation plus the long-term rate of productivity growth, an upward push on the growth rate of wages, achieved by union negotiators, causes higher unemployment if the central bank maintains the previous rate of monetary growth and higher inflation if the "wage push" is accommodated by an acceleration in monetary growth. The acceleration of wage increases in France in 1968 and in the United Kingdom in 1970 appears to have been caused by autonomous noneconomic events rather than by prior movements of prices or money.

Why would a union push up the wage rate if there were a risk that the main consequence would be higher unemployment? First, seniority provisions concentrate most of the impact of higher unemployment on a politically impotent minority of union members. Second, a wage push may increase the real income of workers at the expense of a squeeze on the profits of firms

[17]This argument is formalized in Robert J. Gordon, "The Demand for and Supply of Inflation," *Journal of Law and Economics*, vol. 18, no. 3, December 1975, pp. 807–836. Examples of particular historical episodes are provided in Charles Maier, "The Political Contexts of Inflation: A Comparative Analysis," unpublished paper presented at the Cliometrics Conference, Madison, Wisc., April 10–12, 1975.

producing internationally traded goods, since foreign competition prevents these firms from raising prices in response to a domestic wage push. Third, although a wage push that is accommodated by the central bank and is accompanied by an exchange depreciation may push up the price level as much as wages, preventing any real wage gain, nevertheless union members will tend to gain a larger share of income relative to owners of fixed-income assets (bonds and savings accounts).

A labor union wage push is just one of the several possible types of supply shocks that can raise the price level required for business firms to be willing to produce the economy's natural level of output. A crop failure or an increase in the price of oil may also, as we have seen, create pressure on the monetary authority to print the additional money needed to finance the higher prices of transactions at the natural output level. A refusal by the central bank to accommodate a supply shock creates an output recession and an increase in unemployment, as happened worldwide during the 1974–1976 period.

Nations with a large share of output produced by nationalized industries are particularly vulnerable to wage-push pressure, as both the British and Italian cases demonstrate. When their prices are held down by government regulation, nationalized industries almost guarantee the accommodation of a wage push, which raises nationalized industry deficits and forces the central government to increase the growth of the money supply to finance these larger deficits. In this sense the demand for monetary accommodation from governmental deficits interacts with the demand originating in private cost pressures.

THE SUPPLY OF MONETARY ACCOMMODATION

The basic political source of pressure for monetary accommodation is the potential loss of votes which the incumbents in government will suffer if nonaccommodation raises the unemployment rate. This fundamental fact explains why central bankers sometimes "ratify" the inflation originating in wage push or supply shocks and why a new set of personalities at the central bank, as in the United States in 1969–1971, does not necessarily cut the growth of money by the amount necessary to get rid of an inflation inherited from a previous regime. Several economists have built full-fledged theories of the "political business cycle" in which politicians take advantage of the myopia of voters and regularly expand the economy to win votes immediately before the election. In parliamentary systems of the British type, incumbents have the extra advantage of being able to call an election at the optimum time during an economic boom.[18]

Two major sets of factors, one economic and one political, tend to determine the degree of accommodation by different central banks to a given set of pressures for accommodation. First, in nations with short-term labor contracts and frequent wage negotiations, prices and wages tend to respond more quickly to high unemployment, thus cutting short the time required for the private economy by itself to correct unemployment without monetary accommodation. In a nation such as the United States, with three-year wage contracts in the unionized sector and with many other wage agreements pegged explicitly or implicitly to union contracts, many years are necessary for excess unemployment to be eliminated by price flexibility in the absence of government demand stimulus.

A second and more obvious factor encouraging accommodation is an institutional setting that gives the elected government effective day-to-day control over the central bank, in contrast to the long 14-year terms and medium-term independence of the United States Federal Reserve. Even a nominally independent central bank, however, feels pressure to accommodate to some degree, because its independence can be taken away by the legislature and because business bankruptcies caused by non-accommodation expose it to pressure and criticism from its constituency of commercial bankers and business leaders.

Central bankers bear a heavy responsibility when they realize that the degree of wage push is not truly autonomous, but at

[18]A readable discussion of the political hypothesis is contained in Assar Lindbeck, "Stabilization Policy in Open Economies with Endogenous Politicians," *American Economic Review*, vol. 66, May 1976, pp. 1–19.

least to some degree is contingent on the expected response of the central bank. A union that expects a wage push to be accommodated fully, so that no unemployment will occur, is more likely to push than a union that faces the prospect of unemployment for a substantial portion of its membership. It is not inconceivable that the aggressiveness of British and Italian unions and the docility of German and American unions may be at least partly a result of the political control of the central banks in the former countries and the relative independence from political control of central banks in the latter countries. At a deeper level the liberalized unemployment compensation and the full-employment "guarantees" offered by many governments since World War II, in place of the risk of substantial uncompensated unemployment in the prewar era, partially explain why wages are more rigid downward than previously.

The possibility of a mutually reinforcing vicious circle, with a wage push encouraging monetary accommodation, which in turn encourages further episodes of wage push, could potentially cause an ever-accelerating rate of inflation in a floating-exchange-rate regime. Phrased another way, the natural rate of unemployment consistent with nonaccelerating inflation could continuously increase. Some may deny this possibility on the grounds that it has no historical precedent (outside of hyperinflations directly related to wars or located in the peculiar atmosphere of certain Latin American countries). But historical episodes before World War II are irrelevant because our present "fiat money standard," in which money can be issued at a stroke of a governmental pen and is not limited in quantity by the supply of gold, differs fundamentally from the prewar gold standard. In a fiat money standard with a wage-push/monetary accommodation nexus, all bets based on past history are off.

Ironically, floating exchange rates, which one would expect to increase the autonomy of policy and the danger of accelerating inflation, may actually help to keep a wage push under control. First, floating exchange rates untie the domestic currency prices of traded goods from world prices and increase the overall flexibility of the price structure. A central bank that refuses to accommodate will find that floating rates increase the downward adjustment of inflation in response to excess unemployment. Second, floating rates allow the domestic prices of traded goods to respond immediately to a wage push, thus eliminating even a transitory real wage gain for workers. Union leaders may be further inhibited from pushing if every aggressive speech or resolution causes an instantaneous drop in the exchange rate, cutting the real income of labor even *before* the wage negotiations begin.

One suspects that the increased degree of cooperation of British union leaders with wage controls in 1975 and 1976 and their willingness to suffer a decline in real wages resulted from pure fear that the pound would collapse in the absence of union restraint. In fact the pound continued to collapse until North Sea oil came to the rescue in 1977, because central-government deficits created a continued pressure for monetary accommodation and because the British central bank intervened in 1976 to encourage the pound to fall faster than was warranted by domestic conditions. The British example suggests that wage controls in a floating-rate regime may not work without a "deal" between the unions and the central bank which prevents excessive rates of monetary expansion from causing an exchange depreciation and an unanticipated decline in real wages. Pursuing this thought further, the appreciation of the pound in 1977–78, by removal of restraints from trade unions, may prove to be the undoing of wage controls.

THREE

Scenarios for the 1980s

Each decade inherits from its predecessor a set of initial conditions and a "new determination" by policy makers to avoid whatever are widely regarded as the major mistakes of the recent past. For instance, in the late 1940s the set of initial conditions for the United States included expectations of a repetition of the post–World War I deflation, a huge war-created stock of money that made such a deflation impossible, and a new set of attitudes originating in the determination to avoid the trauma of another Great Depression. The 1960s began in the United States with relatively high unemployment, sluggish output growth, and expectations of low rates of inflation, all three the direct result of the restrictive monetary and fiscal policies of the late 1950s. Policy was designed to reduce unemployment and raise output growth but neglected the inevitable rekindling of inflationary expectations that would accompany a return to prosperity. The initial conditions in the 1970s were diametrically opposite—1969 ended with low unemployment and a 5 percent inflation rate, which by then had become built in to expectations and wage contracts. The swing of the political pendulum had swept out the expansionists and brought to power the "gradualists," committed to maintaining slow growth and higher unemployment to damp down the inflation rate.

INITIAL CONDITIONS FOR THE 1980s

The setting of policy in the 1980s obviously depends on that decade's inheritance from the 1970s. As of 1976, it appeared that the legacy of the 1970s for the 1980s would be a slack economy with relatively high unemployment and with an inflation rate that would be decelerating steadily in reaction to the slack conditions. Several surprises in 1977–78, however, have changed that prediction considerably. As a result, the endowment of the 1980s is likely to be considerably more inflation and a tighter labor market than appeared likely just a year or two ago.

The single most important element in this deteriorating endowment is the abysmal performance of the rate of productivity growth during the decade of the 1970s. In the decade ending in mid-1978, the annual growth rate of nonfarm productivity (output per hour) was a modest 1.2 percent, compared to a rate more than twice as high in the earlier postwar period by the United States, and even higher rates achieved by Europe and Japan in the 1970s. The shortfall of productivity growth, which has been attributed at least partly to the influence of environmental, health, and safety legislation, has affected the aggregate inflation-unemployment outlook in two ways. First, the modest growth rate of real output achieved in 1977–78 caused a rapid decline in the unemployment rate from the range of 7.0 percent to 6.0 percent (a decline that was not forecast in 1977 and would not have occurred without the productivity slowdown). Lacking any significant increase in the ability of each worker to produce more output, firms have been forced to hire new workers in massive numbers to cope with growing real sales in 1978.

The second effect of the productivity slowdown has been to contribute to an acceleration of inflation. Many commentators share the view that the fundamental underlying rate of inflation warranted by the behavior of wages and productivity has accelerated from the 6.0 percent range of 1976 and 1977 to a figure of 7.0 or 7.5 percent in 1978. This has occurred not only because the productivity slowdown has boosted the increase in labor cost implicit in each wage negotiation, but also because the wages paid by employers have been pushed up independently by legislated increases in payroll taxes and the minimum wage rate.

Table 1 illustrates several possible scenarios for the 1980s, starting with the situation of 1978. The three "routes" of adjustment are (1) an "expansionist" route, which accepts the inflation of 1978 and refuses to allow any increase in unemployment; (2) a "monetarist" route, which insists on slowing nominal income growth by 1.0 percent per year, thus causing a severe recession; and (3) a "gradualist" route, which allows only a modest increase in unemployment and only a modest deceleration of inflation.

The common elements of each section of Table 1 are the following. First, it is pessimistically assumed that, as a result of the slow growth of productivity, the U.S. economy can attain a growth rate of real output of only 3.0 percent per year when the unemployment rate is held constant. Second, it is assumed that a one-percentage-point *excess* of the rate of real output growth above 3.0 percent per year will reduce the unemployment rate by 0.5 percentage points during that year, and vice versa (this is a modified version of "Okun's Law"). Third, it is assumed that the inflation rate remains steady when unemployment stays constant at 6.0 percent, accelerates if unemployment falls below 6.0 percent, and decelerates if unemployment rises above 6.0 percent. The historical data do not send out clear signals about this "short-run unemployment-inflation tradeoff," but a reasonable guess is that inflation would slow down by half of the percentage-point excess of the unemployment rate over 6.0 percent.

Route 1 exhibits the implications of a constant-growth-rate monetary policy that maintains a 10.0 percent annual growth rate of nominal income throughout the 1979–88 decade. After a deceleration of nominal income and real output growth of one percentage point in 1979, everything remains constant thereafter. This scenario reflects the assumption that the economy enters 1979 with exactly the "natural" amount of unemployment that tends to keep inflation constant, without any acceleration or deceleration. Although route 1 does not achieve any further

TABLE 1
Three Routes by which the United States Economy Might Cope with Inflation, 1978–1988

	Annual Rates of Growth			
	Nominal Income	Inflation Rate	Real Output	Level of Unemployment Rate
Route 1				
1978	11.0	7.0	4.0	6.0
1979	10.0	7.0	3.0	6.0
1980	10.0	7.0	3.0	6.0
1981	10.0	7.0	3.0	6.0
1982	10.0	7.0	3.0	6.0
...	...	...	...	...
1988	10.0	7.0	3.0	6.0
Route 2				
1978	11.0	7.0	4.0	6.0
1979	10.0	7.0	3.0	6.0
1980	9.0	6.5	2.5	6.2
1981	8.0	6.4	1.6	6.9
1982	7.0	5.9	1.1	7.8
1983	6.0	5.0	1.0	8.8
1984	5.0	3.4	1.6	9.5
1985	4.0	1.7	2.3	9.9
1986	3.0	− 0.3	3.3	9.8
1987	3.0	− 2.2	5.2	8.6
1988	3.0	− 3.5	6.5	6.9
Route 3				
1978	11.0	7.0	4.0	6.0
1979	8.5	6.7	1.8	6.6
1980	9.4	6.4	3.0	6.6
1981	9.1	6.1	3.0	6.6
1982	8.8	5.8	3.0	6.6
1983	8.5	5.5	3.0	6.6
...	...	...	...	...
1988	7.0	4.0	3.0	6.6

SOURCE: Author's calculations.

reduction in the overall unemployment rate (pending structural reforms that would make it possible to have less unemployment without an acceleration of inflation), it nevertheless must be classified as relatively expansionist in its failure to pursue an overt policy of slowing down the inflation rate.[19]

Route 2 takes a more conservative approach and is very close to the path recommended by Karl Brunner, Alan Meltzer, and other members of the Fed-watching "Shadow Open Market Committee." It takes literally their recommendation that the growth rate of money (and hence nominal income) be slowed by one percentage point per year, until income growth reaches the 3.0 annual growth rate of real output compatible with constant unemployment. This policy recommendation might induce a slowdown of inflation by the same single percentage point per year under some conditions, but not those governing the operation of the U.S. economy in the late 1970s. In the short run such a monetary deceleration would have little effect on wage demands, particularly in the unionized sector of the economy. Most of the impact of the spending slowdown would be felt by real output and employment, leading to the increases in the unemployment rate shown in the right-hand column. Only gradually, as the high unemployment rates force firms to lower prices and unions to accept more modest wage agreements, would inflation taper off. The specific assumption used here, consistent with recent research on the topic, is that inflation slows each year by half of the percentage-point excess of unemployment above 6.0 percent. For instance, as a consequence of the unemployment rate exceeding 6.0 percent in 1982 by 1.8

[19] What monetary and fiscal policies would yield the growth rates of nominal income shown here? Over the period 1960–77 the growth rates of nominal income and the monetary aggregate "M2" (which includes currency, demand and time deposits) grew at about the same rates, so one presumes that M2 growth rates of roughly the amounts shown in column (1) would be consistent with the policies outlined. The inflation and unemployment outcomes are calculated using the assumptions outlined in the text, together with the fact that real output growth, by definition, is equal to the rate of growth of nominal income minus the inflation rate.

percentage points (7.8 minus 6.0), the inflation rate in 1983 slows by 0.9 percentage points compared to 1982.

Two problems with the monetary deceleration approach are immediately evident. First, a major economic slump is created in which unemployment reaches almost a 10 percent rate in 1985, even though output never literally declines in absolute terms. Second, the policy maintains high unemployment for so long an interval that the inflation rate actually becomes negative. It is evident that route 2 is a purely hypothetical policy that would never be politically acceptable, because of the duration of the slump and the high unemployment rate reached. Trouble develops because the annual slowdown in income growth is faster (at one percentage point per year) than the assumed responsiveness of the inflation rate.

Route 3 achieves a steady deceleration of inflation from 7.0 to 4.0 percent at the cost of only a modest amount of extra unemployment. The policy is not based on achieving an arbitrary annual slowdown in income growth, but rather on allowing the unemployment rate to drift up in 1979 by 0.6 percentage points. By assumption this extra unemployment allows the inflation rate to decelerate by 0.3 percentage points per year. Compared to route 2, this third scenario has the obvious advantage of allowing much more output and employment to occur, a benefit over the 1979–85 interval equal to about $150 billion at the prices of 1978. But the cost is a permanent endowment of 4.0 percent inflation, compared to the much lower (and even negative) inflation rates achieved along route 2. A more subtle advantage of route 3 is that inflation can settle down to a steady rate after 1988, whereas the "overshooting" that occurs along route 2 leads to excessive output growth and oscillations of both inflation and unemployment extending into the 1990s.

Which of these scenarios is the most likely to occur? Or is some other outcome more probable? All three alternatives in Table 1 involve a substantial slowdown in the rate of nominal income growth from the 11 percent pace of 1977 and 1978. During the entire course of 1977 and 1978 the Federal Reserve engineered a very rapid increase in interest rates designed to achieve a slowdown in the growth of money and income. Each previous episode of increasing interest rates—in 1957, 1959,

1966, 1969, and 1973–74—had achieved the desired goal of slowing down income growth. But only in 1966–67 did monetary tightness fail to induce an actual recession (defined as at least two successive quarters of *negative* growth). Thus, on purely historical grounds alone, the Fed's move toward higher interest rates would be expected to cause an increase in unemployment, rather than the steady 6.0 percent unemployment rate depicted along route 1. Also on historical grounds, the Fed is unlikely to maintain the draconian tightness involved in route 2.

Thus route 3 seems the most plausible outcome, although its steady-as-you-go deceleration in the growth of income and prices is probably overoptimistic. In every previous historical episode, the Fed has tightened for too long a period, sent the economy reeling into a steep descent, and then responded by excessive stimulation to undo its previous mistakes. Another factor arguing against a smooth slowdown is the possible reaction of the Congress and the administration to any substantial increase in unemployment. Can those branches of government resist the temptation to engineer a preelection boom in 1980 built on higher spending and cuts in taxes?

Would a fiscal stimulus in late 1979 or 1980, combined with continued monetary discipline, cause a sudden upsurge in the rate of inflation above the pace suggested in Table 1 under route 3? At least initially, little extra inflation would result from a fiscal stimulus, because a tax reduction would allow a gain in real after-tax income without a commensurate increase in before-tax market prices. The fear by Fed governors and their monetarist allies of explosive inflation resulting from higher government deficits neglects three crucial elements of the inflation process. First, the empirical evidence strongly suggests that prices do not live a life of their own (with the exception of a few agricultural commodities and raw materials traded on auction markets) and that the rate of price inflation is basically "pinned down" by the growth in wages adjusted for trend growth in productivity. Second, sudden explosions in wages are unlikely in the United States setting, in which three-year wage contracts dominate the short-term behavior of the average wage index. Third, the huge federal deficits of 1974–1976 did not inhibit the slow but steady deceleration of wage growth. Overall, there is nothing in the behavior of wages in the last 10 years that conflicts with the prediction of the natural-rate hypothesis that the growth of wages will slowly but steadily *slow down*, not speed up, as long as the actual unemployment rate remains above the natural unemployment rate.

A policy mix that combines tight monetary policy with a fiscal stimulus in the late 1970s creates an unfortunate endowment for the 1980s. A temporary tax cut suffers from the handicap discussed above, that households will not raise their estimated permanent income and hence their consumption much if they expect the tax cut to be reversed. Thus a temporary tax cut would have to be very large to achieve a major reduction in unemployment, and this size tax cut would cause a substantial increase in the "natural employment deficit," that is, in the federal deficit that would occur if the economy were operating at the natural rate of unemployment.[20] Further, it may be politically difficult for the administration to rescind the tax cut in the 1981 postelection period, even though the economy may well need restraint at that time to prevent overshooting the natural unemployment rate target.

There is no presumption in economic theory that the natural employment deficit should be zero. In fact it is possible to argue in the abstract that either a deficit or a surplus is optimal.[21] The basic advantage of a surplus is that government saving adds to rather than subtracts from the amount of private saving available to finance private investment. The long period of high unemployment and low capacity utilization in the mid-1970s has caused a slump in investment spending. Since there has been no compensating factor to hold down growth in the labor force, the 1980s will inherit a capital stock that is growing at an unusually slow speed relative to the labor force. Although the main effect of slow capital growth will be to hold down the growth of

[20] The much publicized "full-employment surplus" is overly optimistic, because it is based on the unrealistic assumption that the economy can attain a 4 percent unemployment rate without continuously accelerating inflation.

[21] Martin J. Bailey, "The Optimal Full-Employment Surplus," *Journal of Political Economy,* July/August 1972, pp. 649–661.

productivity, an additional and more serious consequence is the real possibility that we will lack sufficient productive capacity in certain basic materials industries, particularly steel, aluminum, and paper, requiring some combination of rationing and steep price increases.[22] Fiscal stimulation in the late 1970s would raise interest rates, crowd out some investment projects, and aggravate a problem we are likely to face anyway.

One possible mitigating element is suggested by our earlier discussion of the "demand for monetary accommodation." A higher federal deficit resulting from fiscal stimulation would create an extra pressure for monetary accommodation. The Federal Reserve is likely to offset at least part of the increase in the level of interest rates caused by the higher deficit by raising the rate of monetary growth. Thus fiscal stimulation in the preelection period of 1980 would make it more difficult for the Fed to achieve the gradual slowdown of income growth depicted along route 3, and this factor pushing the Fed toward another round of stimulation introduces one element that makes the projected slowdown of inflation along route 3 look overly optimistic. Floating exchange rates make this monetary response to fiscal stimulation less likely than under the old Bretton Woods system, however, since monetary accommodation by the Fed now brings with it a depreciation of the dollar and pressure on the domestic inflation rate.

THE POTENTIAL FOR A NEW ROUND OF SURPRISES

Perhaps the most startling aspect of the three routes displayed in Table 1, in contrast to current conventional journalistic wisdom, is that inflation in the 1980s should be no higher than in 1978 with each of the three policies. In fact the situation in the late-1980s looks positively blissful from this vantage point, a contrast that should not be at all surprising. First, the long period of high

---

[22] For a recent evaluation of this possibility, see the printed conference discussion of Barry Bosworth, "Capacity Creation in the Basic Materials Industries," *Brookings Papers on Economic Activity*, vol. 7, no. 2, 1976.

unemployment during the 1970s has fundamentally been an investment in inflation fighting. Like any investment, the sacrifice comes now, in the form of lost jobs, wasted machinery, lower profits, less consumption, and less capital accumulation. The payoff from the investment will come later in the form of lower inflation. Whatever the arguments for and against this form of investment, there is no doubt that in 1975–1977 the entire industrialized world chose a path of great current sacrifice. It would indeed be rather pathetic if the entire process were in vain; thus inflation in the mid-1980s *above* the rates of the mid-1970s would be truly surprising.

A second argument supporting the optimism of Table 1 is the predominant role of unprecedented supply shocks, particularly the oil-price increase, in creating the high inflation of 1973–1975. Oil prices will rise again, but not by 400 percent within one year. The events of 1973–1975 were unprecedented, and there is no presumption that another upheaval must occur in the 1980s. During the early 1950s many people expected that, because we had experienced two world wars during the first half of this century, we would necessarily suffer from at least one more during the last half of the century, but a third world war looks considerably less likely now than it did even 15 years ago. There were no major demand or supply shocks during the 1952–1965 interval, and we sometimes forget the long stretch of tranquil decades in the nineteenth century which passed without major wars or supply shocks.

Nevertheless we must consider the possibility of one or more major surprises, which would prevent the achievement of stable growth in the 1980s at a relatively low inflation rate, beyond the inherent instability of route 2 pointed out above. The first possibility is that the growth of wage rates will not slow down as rapidly as assumed in Table 1. A slower wage deceleration would delay the economy's arrival at lower inflation rates, and would raise the unemployment and output cost of any given investment in inflation fighting. The precedent of 1956–1964 is reassuring: the rate of change of wages decelerated steadily from 1956 to 1964 even during the economic expansion of 1961–1964. Only after the economy passed rapidly below the natural rate of unemployment, during 1965, did wage change begin to accelerate. The best protection against a wage acceleration is to prevent unemployment from falling below 6 percent.

There is no more important assumption in this paper than that wage rates are heavily influenced by the inertia created by three-year contracts and that wage change will slow down relative to expected inflation and productivity growth as long as the actual unemployment rate remains above the natural rate. As a result, the danger of an acceleration in wages can be ignored as long as actual unemployment remains high. This sanguine approach is *not* recommended for nations with other sets of labor-market institutions. As Arthur Okun has remarked, "Every foreigner that comes to my office just cannot understand how the United States can have such a different kind of wage behavior. They always ask when we are going to have our wage explosion. It is not even whether. It is when."[23] Okun and others who are nervous rather than sanguine about the possibility of a United States wage explosion in response to aggregate demand stimulation place heavy emphasis on a government–labor union "social contract" that would trade lower unemployment and tax reductions for union promises to maintain moderate wage growth. I see little harm in attempting to implement this approach but have little hope that it could be implemented without distorting price controls as well.

Major supply shocks might upset the scenarios of Table 1. Crop failures are always a possibility and call for government policy intervention, as outlined below. But the major damage of higher oil prices has been done. An annual increase in oil prices equal to our domestic rate of inflation has no more impact than an equal percentage increase in the price of clothing or shoes. Even a 15 percent annual rate of increase in the price of oil would add 0.5 percentage points or less to the domestic United States inflation rate (less if "old oil" prices are controlled). A uniform oil-import tariff adopted by all the industrialized na-

[23] United States Congress, House and Senate, Joint Economic Committee, *Midyear Review of the Economic Situation and Outlook,* 94th Congress, 2d session, June 1976, p. 73.

tions, as recently proposed by Hendrik Houthakker, would provide a bargaining tool that might moderate the rate of OPEC oil-price increases even further.

Supply shocks imposed by producer cartels in markets of other imported raw materials cannot cause major problems, simply because there is nothing else comparable to oil in either dollar importance or in the absence of substitutes. The most unfortunate "price surprises" may not originate abroad but may be caused by shortages of capacity in our own domestic basic materials producing industries.

But at least two other factors call for caution in taking too literally the scenarios laid out in Table 1 and for assigning some weight to the possibility that the inflation-unemployment problem will be more intractable. First, in the late 1970s the United States government has introduced measures that are analytically similar to supply shocks—by raising business costs, they tend simultaneously to make inflation and unemployment worse. Among these measures are substantial increases in social security payroll taxes, energy taxes, and the minimum wage planned for the 1978–1981 period. To the extent that these measures are actually put into effect, the government has only itself to blame for "legislated inflation." These measures could raise the annual rate of inflation by at least a full percentage point during each year of the 1978–1981 period, compared with the entries in Table 1.

Second, there are two important factors that could cause a temporary *acceleration* of inflation in 1979–80 even with the slowdown in income growth depicted along routes 2 and 3. The first of these is the delayed impact of the dramatic decline in the value of the U.S. dollar between mid-1977 and late 1978. In principle this weakness in the dollar should have pushed up prices relative to wages as it occurred, not just as a direct result of the higher prices of imports, but also as a result of the opportunity for wider profit margins on domestic products that compete with imports. As of late 1978 this "pass-through" of the effects of dollar depreciation had not yet occurred to any great extent, leaving a delayed impact for 1979 as a time bomb in the inflation outlook. To the extent that an acceleration of inflation in 1979 causes negotiated wage changes to speed up rather than slow down, the inflation inherited in the early 1980s would be more rapid than is depicted in Table 1. The second time bomb is the delayed impact of the abysmal productivity growth recorded by the U.S. economy in the decade of the 1970s. If workers still attempt to achieve a 2.5 or 3.0 pecent annual improvement in real wages while the economy's ability to pay (in the form of growing productivity) rises at only 1.0 or 1.5 percent, continuing upward pressure will be placed on the inflation rate. In sum, the behavior of the dollar and of productivity during 1978 has shifted the balance toward the pessimistic conclusion that achieving a deceleration in inflation may be an even more difficult and protracted process than that laid out in Table 1.

POLICY PRIORITIES TO ACHIEVE STEADY LOW-INFLATION GROWTH IN THE 1980s

Monetarists and nonmonetarists agree that the Federal government should issue an indexed bond and that nominal elements of the tax structure, particularly tax brackets, exemptions, and the standard deduction, should be tied to a broad price index. Adoption of these proposals would substantially reduce the benefit to society of a "hard-line" anti-inflationary policy such as route 2 in Table 2 and would strengthen the case for the less draconian route 3.

At this point monetarists and nonmonetarists part company. Most monetarists agree that a constant growth-rate rule monetary policy, as along route 1, is inappropriate if the economy begins in a disequilibrium situation, and they support something on the order of route 2. In their view no further discussion of policy is required, and so the additional policy recommendations listed below reveal my nonmonetarist bias.

The magnitude of the billions of output both in the United States and abroad wasted in a route-2-recession, taken together with the possibility of providing a government-indexed bond to minimize the costs of the higher permanent inflation rate along route 3, leads me to endorse leaning toward the latter scenario.

Among the many reasons for opposing route 2 is the positive *harm* of returning to complete price stability! Since the mid-1960s billions have been borrowed at high interest rates that have at least partially reflected a positive expected rate of inflation, and price stability would redistribute a substantial amount of income from debtors to creditors.

Avoiding a major recession in the late 1970s imposes on the 1980s the permanent cost of faster inflation but the permanent benefit of a larger capital stock. The United States tax system interposes a substantial wedge between the before-tax rate of return on capital and the after-tax rate of return on saving, thus cutting the overall propensity to save below the optimal level. An extra dollar of saving produces a rate of return for society that substantially exceeds the cost to the marginal saver of postponing consumption. Thus another argument in favor of route 3 is that the higher resulting 1980s' capital stock moves society in the right direction toward a higher optimal capital-output ratio.

The choice of policy instruments during the transition period should also be governed by the goal of encouraging saving and investment. This goal creates an impetus for shifting the mix of policy toward easier money and tighter fiscal policy, but political realities push in the opposite direction and are sure to dominate in the short to medium run. Thus the required fiscal stimulus should be designed to encourage investment and discourage consumption. A straightforward income or payroll tax cut slanted toward low-income families would work in exactly the wrong direction.

The general principle guiding the design of fiscal incentives should be to stimulate spending that (1) creates jobs when there is slack in the economy and (2) leaves the economy with a long-run benefit after the spending stops. An attractive fiscal package would combine the following four elements.

First, a Swedish-type countercyclical investment fund, which requires firms to set aside profits during boom years which are made available to finance investment projects during slack years. One possibility would be an "unemployment-contingent investment subsidy," which would underwrite projects by a percentage that varies with the unemployment rate. The inflationary impact of such a subsidy can be minimized by channeling it largely to regions with above-average unemployment rates. Unlike a temporary income tax cut, which may have only a minor impact on consumption, a temporary cut in sales taxes or increase in subsidies creates a powerful incentive to shift the timing of expenditures.

Second, in periods of high unemployment the United States government should take advantage of low industrial-capacity utilization by buying a stockpile of basic raw materials that are most likely to run into capacity shortages when lower rates of unemployment are reached. A more radical scheme would have the government actually build additional plant capacity for these "problem industries," with the intention of selling the plants to existing firms when the economy expands enough to require the extra capacity.

Third, the government can mitigate the effect of future agricultural supply shocks by systematically purchasing stocks of major commodities when harvests are good and prices are relatively low.

Finally, just as the government can spend money now to avoid a steel shortage in the 1980s, so it can spend to avoid a skills shortage. In the previous discussion the natural unemployment rate is taken as fixed at roughly 6.0 percent in the United States. But this high level of the natural unemployment rate results partly from a mismatch between the high level of skills required by many job openings and the low level of skills possessed by most of those who remain unemployed when the economy is at the natural rate of unemployment. To overcome this problem a mixture of programs is likely to be more efficient than a single doctrinaire approach. The programs should include training subsidies to private firms, relocation subsidies such as those recently instituted in West Germany, a better employment service, and a program to provide income-contingent loans to finance vocational training.

Government deficits generated by these programs would not crowd out private investment if investment is stimulated by the higher levels of capacity utilization that will result from the fiscal stimulus. In addition, government deficits used to finance productive investments in physical or human capital do not squeeze out capital spending but merely shift the source of financing and the particular type of capital that is accumulated.

INTERNATIONAL ASPECTS OF THE DOMESTIC POLICY PRESCRIPTIONS

Most small nations in the world are waiting for the tide of world economic recovery to raise their own little ships, because they lack the policy autonomy to stimulate themselves. The major industrialized countries are divided into two groups. The first consists of Britain, Italy, and to a lesser extent France and is characterized by a struggle to escape from a vicious circle of government deficits, excessive monetary expansion, exchange depreciation, inflation, and explosive wage increases. The demand for and supply of monetary accommodation interact with a hypersensitive foreign-exchange market, and a continued policy of austerity is inescapable. Only in Britain is a moderate stimulus made possible, by the tapping of North Sea oil. The second group of countries consists mainly of Germany and Japan; both are terrified by the victimization of the first group under the new regime of floating exchange rates, and determined to avoid the same fate by resisting any major policy stimulus. They are also eager to resist further exchange appreciation in order to maintain existing export-market shares.

The inflation rates in the two groups of countries have spread far enough apart to guarantee that the floating-rate system is here to stay and that nothing resembling fixed rates will return during the 1980s. The volatility of exchange rates since 1973 reflects a huge pool of mobile international capital that would rapidly undermine any attempt to fix the exchange rates between major industrialized countries. The behavior of exchange rates since 1973 and the trauma of double-digit inflation appear together to have combined to paralyze economic policy making in the large countries. Few would have predicted five years ago that the movement to floating rates would create such a bias in the system toward higher unemployment and against demand stimulation.

The impotence of the small countries and the need for austerity in the group of large "invalid" nations leaves the responsibility for world recovery with the United States, Germany, and Japan. This adds a weighty additional argument to the case for avoiding excessive restriction in the United States, for a major recession in the United States, together with the inability of the weaker nations to pursue growth-oriented policies, could drag down the world economy into another worldwide recession. In 1976 and 1977 the United States alone pursued expansionary policies, and because these were not matched by Germany and Japan, the consequence was a plummeting dollar and an exacerbation of the U.S. inflation problem. In late 1978 the United States finds itself, much sooner than anyone predicted, already at its "natural" unemployment rate, representing an effective limit on the further pursuit of expansionary policies. Opinion inside the United States is virtually unanimous that a temporary period of slower growth is needed to lower the inflation rate, with the major differences represented by the contrast between routes 2 and 3 in Table 1. As a result, responsibility for continuing the pace of worldwide economic growth falls more than ever to Germany and Japan. Fortunately, policy-makers in these strong nations have become alarmed by the precipitous decline in the dollar and now have even more incentive than before to keep their economies growing, because the strength of their currencies has allowed their inflation to drop off to negligible rates. The modest restriction involved in a route 3 policy for the United States, combined with more rapid growth in Germany and Japan, should eventually allow the dollar to recover and thereby amplify the downward pressure on the U.S. inflation rate created by the projected "mini-recession" of 1979–80.

Economic Cooperation among Western Countries

Jacques Pelkmans

ONE

Domestic Politics and International Economic Cooperation

The economic health of the West in the postwar period was due in many ways to progress in international economic cooperation. Today we constantly hear of this ongoing process through economic summits and special negotiations. The shape of the 1980s and, in particular, the vigor of the Western economies in the future depend on the continued success of this cooperation. Thus, a detailed analysis of its potential problems and structure is critical to an informed understanding of the medium-term future. Before improved methods of cooperation can be prescribed, a clearer picture of the current modes of policy cooperation and the limitations implicit in them is needed. Such an analysis is also the purpose of this paper. As a grounding for this study I will look at the domestic politics of Western nations in terms of their fundamental economic goals and the conflicts that these produce. The core of the paper is an analysis of international economic cooperation that distinguishes between various forms of cooperation and examines their limitations. I conclude with a brief assessment of the kinds of cooperation that are needed and likely in the future.

DOMESTIC POLITICS AND ECONOMIC POLICY

In the Western industrialized world the drift away from the principles of laissez faire, embodied in nineteenth-century liberalism, grew mainly out of ever more ambitious economic goals. On a very general level this broadening of the goals of economic policy is related to a gradual evolution in basic views of the aims of society—emphasizing individual freedom, social justice, welfare, independence, and stability. Although it has been recognized since Adam Smith that the free functioning of markets is theoretically capable of assuring aims such as global welfare, skepticism arose over the achievement of such goals as social justice, national independence, and the stability of markets. Economic policies have over the years attempted to respond to this skepticism. In addition, since perfect competition has always been elusive, policies have been initiated to correct inefficient and restrictive market behavior as displayed, for example, by oligopolies.

The economic goals of Western industrialized countries fit into general hierarchical policy structures, which give a relative status to virtually all goals. Western societies embody a set of fundamental values or aims. Some countries emphasize individual freedom; others, by contrast, put more emphasis on social justice and equity. To some degree they also attempt to realize goals of welfare, independence, stability, democracy, and the principle of the rule of law. Obviously, this list is not exhaustive and the hierarchies vary among countries. In the effort to achieve such aims these societies are all structured by constitutions and laws that leave the formulation of policy up to the majority.

Economic policies are directly related to the hierarchy of aims and their articulation by the majority. They are, however, usually named by their objective, as in a full-employment policy, a price-stabilization policy, an exchange-rate policy, an economic growth policy, etc. These objectives are achieved by manipulating *instruments*, which are such things as taxes, tariffs, government spending, and subsidies. Instruments can sometimes be secondary objectives; for example, a low interest rate can be instrumental in stimulating economic growth but it can also directly serve equity purposes by lowering the income of capital holders. Economic policies are intrinsically *political* because domestic political preferences, in the form of national aims expressed by the majority, are the driving force behind their initiation and implementation.

The basic political nature of economic policies is normally concealed by the tendency to discuss them as technical issues, on the level of instruments, or in terms of the short- and long-run effectiveness of various instruments. Only rarely is the actual relation between objectives and aims spelled out in the process of economic policy making. Perhaps this relationship is kept implicit because it is felt that economic science quickly recedes into the background when linked to hierarchies of values or because tradition teaches the economist to accept the political foundation of economics as a separate, noneconomic system that is exogenously given. This tradition has been carried over from laissez faire economic thought, but its status is dubious on a globe where the Second and the Third Worlds explicitly proclaim the subservience of economics to politics and even the First World has sharply departed from the principles of nonintervention in markets and unrestricted private initiative.

The political nature of economic policies can also be concealed by domestic institutional preferences. If, for example, economic policies seek to strengthen the functioning of markets and conform to their mechanisms rather than restrict them, there is implicit in such policies a fundamental political decision in favor of individual economic freedom. According to Katzenstein, these institutional preferences result in part from the country's domestic structure and are of critical importance for the type of policy that is followed. In comparing France and the United States, he concludes, "State-centered policy networks in France facilitate the pursuit of political objectives; society-centered networks in the United States give free play to the quest for economic aims,"[1] or a more general and somewhat extreme characterization, "government policies are shaped not by the character of the issue but by the constraints of domestic structures."[2]

The relation between domestic politics and economic policy is much more complex, however, than simply the pervasive influence of institutional preferences that Katzenstein proposes. Taking a short-run view, there are at least three additional, direct

[1]Peter Katzenstein, "International Relations and Domestic Structures: Foreign Economic Policies of Advanced Industrial States," *International Organization*, vol. 30, Winter 1976, p. 21.
[2]Ibid., p. 43.

linkages between domestic politics and economic policy making. The first originates from *constituency politics* because specific economic policy decisions are sometimes taken or postponed to satisfy particular interest groups that have special influence with politicians. Constituency politics are a classic determinant of policies in the microeconomic sphere and thus are critical for antitrust policies, foreign trade and investment policies, or agricultural policies. For example, in the United States rural states are overrepresented in the Senate with respect to their total share of population, creating a "green bloc" that significantly influences the shape of agricultural policy.

The second linkage can be found in *electoral politics* because both the executive and the members of the legislature will usually act in a way that enhances the probability of reelection. To a significant extent, this can overlap with constituency politics for, say, the individual politician in Parliament or Congress. For the government as a whole an endless series of piecemeal policy measures concerning small groups of people does not have great appeal. Governments tend to conceive electorates as broader and less segmented than politicians, who are chosen by regions, districts, or proportions of the electorate. Electoral politics, as opposed to constituency politics, may be considered a critical influence on macroeconomic policies, such as monetary and fiscal policy, exchange-rate policy, and policies of income distribution. To give a striking short-run example, electoral politics can easily produce a tax reduction in the fiscal year before an election.

The third linkage is caused by overload of the policy system and consists of *trade-off politics*. The economic policy system contains a multitude of conflicting instruments and goals that require political choices to resolve their differences, which sometimes even means the creation of new, often more interventionist, instruments. Consider the following examples: sectoral tariff protection helps preserve jobs but enrages trade partners; the benefits of less inflation have to be traded off against the benefits of more employment; the benefits of a low exchange rate, namely to encourage exports, also make imports more expensive, which can be disastrous if a country is heavily dependent on foreign oil. In all these examples political choices have to be made which are hard on politicians. In the case of tariffs, avoiding protection and opting for adjustment assistance could be felt as yet another burden on the taxpayers. In the inflation-unemployment dilemma policy makers want the best of all worlds, but it is next to impossible to suppress both high inflation and unemployment in the short run. Here success lies in the medium term, and this does not improve reelection chances.

Governments have also attempted to introduce new instruments, such as wage and price controls, to bring down the rate of inflation. In trade-off politics the issue is not so much the economic merits of controls but rather the fact that controls mean a shift away from a market-oriented economy. It is important to note that controls are mainly a political issue because inflation can also be fought by checking the growth of the domestic money supply, implying adjustments by borrowers, and a suppression of investment.

In brief, the scope and shape of economic policy is strongly influenced by domestic politics, both fundamentally and in daily affairs. This conclusion tends to be neglected or minimized in economic writings about policy problems. This interaction between politics and the creation of economic policies fosters the formulation of *ad hoc policies* and a strong bias toward *short-run policies*, which give results *within* the governing period and improve an incumbent's election prospects. Such tendencies are easily justifiable to the politician but are often upsetting to the economist. In times of high expectations among citizens, politicians must gain support by means of competitive promises of policy output with respect to all objectives that are nationally recognized. With respect to some major economic objectives, they merely "sell" a differentiated product, that is, they try to accomplish similar policy aims by promising to use different policy instruments that appeal to different groups of voters.

ECONOMIC SECURITY AND POLITICIZATION

Over the last century Western societies have increasingly sought economic security. This search is probably the most important force behind the increased salience and range of economic policies. Economic security is to a certain extent a subjective notion and escapes definition as an unambiguous concept. In addition, it also denotes slightly different things at different levels of analysis.

For the *individual* citizen economic security consists in the assurance of living beyond bare subsistence, even if a job is not available or the person is unable to work. For the *nation*, it refers to the political obligation of the government to ensure an acceptable level of economic growth and stability while also providing a reasonable distribution of welfare. Of course, what is considered to be "reasonable" and "acceptable" is determined by domestic politics and the level of economic development. For a large *group of nations*, or the world as a whole, economic security means the stability of international economic relations, particularly the assurance of crucial imported supplies, access to markets for exports, and the general level of national economic openness. As a result, economic security is strongly influenced by international political relations—especially through perceptions of national interest and confidence in the policies of other governments.

One can conceive of the search for economic security on these various levels as a reaction to the liberalism of the nineteenth century. In Western Europe the achievement of general suffrage and high levels of literacy has undoubtedly enhanced political awareness and strengthened social and political organizations aimed at improving the lot of workers and peasants. Even in the United States, where there was an abundance of opportunities to transcend subsistency, Roosevelt's New Deal and Johnson's Great Society responded to the desire for more stable and certain patterns of life.

Until the 1930s, government intervention to satisfy political demands for economic security was believed to be harmful by the majority of economists. It still is by many. But there is a definite political element to it that should be spelled out. In a democracy, voters can express dissatisfaction with current economic arrangements. It may be that citizens in the Western world are displaying an *increasing preference for economic security* that competes with and perhaps at times even transcends the usually presumed incentive of private welfare maximization. This preference may indeed be the underlying cause for the rising importance of economic policy. The emergence of economic security as a supreme preference of citizens also explains the fear governments have of enforcing downward economic adjustments, which are sure to be politically unpopular.

The Quest for Individual Economic Security

A pervasive instrument in the quest for individual economic security has been the establishment and gradual extensions of social security systems. Today, social security systems in Western countries guarantee all people subsistence levels of food, shelter, health care, and clothing. The other basic instrument for providing individuals with a sense of economic security has been full-employment policies. The application of these two instruments has virtually eliminated the desperately poor in most industrialized countries. However, the quest for individual economic security has raised expectations, producing at least three undesirable repercussions.

First, the degree of intersectoral and interregional mobility of labor has decreased substantially. The realization by citizens that pockets of unemployment can be eliminated by political pressure rather than by market adjustment does not motivate people to move to find new jobs. Relatively high employment allowances also weaken the incentive for retraining, making labor more reluctant to change sectors. For technologically advanced industries and for the service sector, the costs of creating economies of scale tend to be so large that investment capital decreasingly responds to great regional differences in its scarcity. Although only the first two bear a clear relationship to the quest for individual economic security, diminutions of factor mobility create greater resistance to microeconomic adjustment and thus make full-employment policies more difficult to achieve.

Second, there is a tendency to individualize the full-employment objective by striving for job and tenure security rather than the security of employment. To be sure, such tendencies are stronger in Japan and Western Europe than in the United States.

Combining this tendency with the well-known downward rigidity of wages, it is clear that the structural rate of unemployment can be easily forced upward, imposing great fiscal burdens on the economy for the support of these unemployed workers. Attempts to obtain job or tenure security are obviously expressions of the increased unwillingness to conform to market adjustment.

Third, the concern for individual economic security has sharply increased the sensitivity of workers in declining industries to the increased unemployment and relative stagnation of wages in these sectors. The typical response is a joint effort by management and labor to resist disinvestment and layoffs that are necessary for market adjustment. Instead demands are made for protection, subsidies, and exemption from indirect taxes to boost the position of the industry at the expense of economic efficiency.

The achievement of individual economic security eventually increases resistance to market adjustment processes and, more specifically, to market-imposed adjustment processes. In times of general economic growth, such resistance is generally concealed and adjustments are either voluntary, induced by salary and career opportunities elsewhere, or unnecessary because even marginal firms can prosper. During downswings and periods of structural stagnation—as in the mid-1970s—adjustment is harshly imposed by the market and strong resistance may develop. Resistance might be organized by labor unions or voiced by local politicians, eventually producing noticeable political pressure on the level of constituency politics and increasing the politicization of economic policies.

This sequence of events contains an important lesson. Security is basically conservative. The provision of individual economic security, especially by means of ambitious employment policies, has produced a strong desire for job continuity that runs counter to the flexible adjustment processes integral to a dynamic economy. In this way, simple policies of transfers and government expenditure that do not interfere with the structure of markets in the short run can eventually provoke politicization and resistance to market forces through their impact on individual economic security and thus significantly complicate economic policy making.

The Quest for National Economic Security

During the 1950s and 1960s, most OECD countries attempted to promote national economic security by maneuvering within the so-called magic square, consisting of policies for full employment, economic growth, price stability, and balance-of-payments equilibrium. Full-employment policies, in addition to their direct impact on individual economic security, also contribute to national economic security by supporting a stable sociopolitical climate. In the post–World War II period, national economic security has been strengthened primarily by vigorous growth policies that have led to great improvements in the standard of living and by the advent of mass consumption societies. For reasons of social justice and political stability, income distribution policies were initiated. This redistribution was relatively easy because economic growth allowed room for equity through the division of income increments. Adding to the prevailing sense of security were low levels of inflation, which ensured the smooth functioning of capital markets and allowed the pegging of all major currencies to the United States dollar, which in turn facilitated international trade and finance. For this reason, internal balance (full employment at stable prices) and external balance (balance-of-payments equilibrium under pegged exchange rates) conflicted only mildly, thus eliminating another barrier to continuous welfare improvement.

However, this quest for national economic security also produced several ironic and peculiar repercussions. In the first place, governments became more concerned about national economic security the more they helped provide it. The recent decades of economic growth and nationally distributed prosperity increased the economic openness of all Organization for Economic Cooperation and Development (OECD) countries, undoubtedly contributing to economic growth through export demand and direct investment as well as greater efficiency due to economies of scale and import competition. But at the same time economic openness loosened the grip of policy makers on their economies, thus undermining their ability to provide national economic security. This is not to say that the actual performance of a national

79

economy will necessarily deteriorate because of openness but merely that the actual performance of a national economy is less securely protected from international disturbances.

Two important political corollaries follow from this observation. Domestically, it becomes harder for the government to preserve the confidence of the legislature and, ultimately, the electorate. With increased economic openness, these groups are more and more sensitive to the influences that foreign production and consumption have on the country. The classic example is when foreign goods become more competitive and take a larger share of the domestic market away from indigenous producers. This situation eventually is likely to give rise to demands for decreased exposure to world markets. Internationally, economic interdependence tends to increase every nation's stake in the maintenance of stable international economic relations. Take, for example, the increasing demands for energy in the OECD area, which lead to dependence on imported oil. Apart from the happy few—Norway, Canada, and recently Great Britain—all OECD countries are heavy importers of oil and some of natural gas, which makes them extremely dependent on OPEC. Of course, some OPEC members have ambitious development plans, so the relationship between OECD and OPEC seems to be one of symbiosis rather than direct conflict. For the OECD countries, however, the structural dependence on energy imports necessarily makes international political issues out of questions of oil supply security and price stability.

Another important repercussion of the quest for national economic security is that continued economic growth and virtually full employment up until the early 1970s raised the level of expectations among citizens and politicians. Among voters growing expectations created less tolerance for failures in the achievement of given objectives and hardened resistance to normal market adjustment processes. This became apparent in the 1970s just when much higher energy bills, the exhaustion of market enlargement possibilities in Western Europe, and lower military and space expenditures necessitated modesty in policy aspirations and downward adjustment in various national economies.

So the growth of expectations was in direct conflict with the necessary economic slowdown. On the other hand, politicians attempted to win elections by competing in their promises to voters and pressure groups, often overcommitting themselves.

Eventually, given the economic constraints of the period, governments ran up against some extremely difficult political choices between such things as internal or external balance, low inflation or low unemployment, higher economic growth or better social services, and higher growth or a less polluted environment, to mention only a few. The reluctance of governments to face these dilemmas directly and the increased resistance of voters, pressure groups, and political parties to accept macroeconomic adjustment found their expression in rapidly increasing rates of inflation fueled by the quadrupling of oil prices. In effect, trade-off politics caused governments to limit their pursuit of price stability and to take a less disciplined approach to the external balance by adopting flexible exchange rates.

It should be noted that even tougher political choices were avoided because the worldwide inflation was financed partly by the dollar overhang that existed after the United States decision to take the dollar off the gold standard in 1971 and partly by the efficient recycling of petrodollars in Western capital markets. Only the persistence of dismal forecasts for the overall OECD economy and the subsequent acceptance of austerity gradually reduced political resistance to adjustment and anti-inflationary policies. In such a climate, governments could begin to publicly target a rate of growth for the domestic money supply, thus limiting in advance political and social claims.

The above analysis suggests that the effort to provide national economic security is even more politicized than the quest for individual security. In particular, strong political resistance to macroeconomic adjustment has in fact been cultivated by the very success of economic policies in the OECD economies. Furthermore, specialization, today's large scale of production, and massive needs for both sophisticated inputs and energy have improved the performances of national economies but at the same time have increased their economic openness and their vulnerability to international disturbances. Thus national economic security is directly linked to the political and economic management of the world economy.

The Quest for International Economic Security

Given their degree of economic openness, countries regard international economic security as a function of the stability of critical imports, in terms of prices and supplies and the reliability of access to crucial markets. Although there are objective elements in the concepts of import stability and export reliability, an important determinant of a nation's sense of security is subjective.

Perceptions can differ widely among countries for many reasons. For example, in a high-demand situation, exporters of raw materials feel secure and are indifferent to the desire of importers for price stability or supply guarantees. Governments of countries with a large industrial sector often perceive their exposure to competitive imports from semi-industrialized countries as sufficient cause to protect national markets and thus maintain sectoral employment. This, of course, ignores the concerns of the exporting country that, as a result, can no longer maintain employment in its export sector. Even countries with similar structures of international trade can differ in their perceptions of security. For example, while France and the United States were both modest energy importers, the French saw this as a source of insecurity and attempted to reduce energy dependence whereas the United States has until very recently displayed only minimal concern over its growing dependence on imported oil.

For OECD countries, international economic security in the postwar period has been maintained through a system that was initiated, stimulated, and, with some important reservations, sustained by the United States.[3] This world economic order was characterized by relatively free trade in industrial products, mod-

[3]For an interesting essay on this subject, see Hirsch and Doyle in Fred Hirsch, Michael W. Doyle, and Edward L. Morse, *Alternatives to Monetary Disorder*, McGraw-Hill for the Council on Foreign Relations/1980s Project, New York, 1977, pp. 11–64.

erate or only temporary restrictions on flows of both portfolio and direct investment, and a general stability in exchange rates. The stability of import prices—a key element of international economic security—resulted from stable exchange rates and a heavy reliance on multilateral trading, which increased international competition.

Trade was enhanced by the creation of a multilateral trade arrangement in the General Agreement on Tariffs and Trade (GATT) based on the principle that all countries, regardless of size or influence, subject themselves to a common set of trade rules so that the reliability of export markets could be substantially increased. In the agreement's ideal form, considerations of domestic or international politics would be eliminated as factors in trade policy, thus giving free sway to international market forces. To make the agreement acceptable and practical, the founding members included a multitude of escape clauses and exceptions. To prevent the erosion of the GATT, unilaterally invoked exceptions and escape clauses were, in principle, made subject to multilateral surveillance. This attempt at world trade management assumes that national trade policies are an international issue and more than just a national concern. The members of the GATT thus enhanced their international economic security and consequently the willingness of participants to further intensify international economic intercourse to the benefit of all. In addition, by setting detailed rules for these agreements, they made trade policy more of a technical international question.

A similar approach was followed with the world monetary system. A system of pegged rates with ample possibilities for financing temporary balance-of-payments deficits sought to assure the stability of exchange rates. In addition to using central bank reserves, deficits could be financed by one or more credit tranches from the International Monetary Fund (IMF). With the provision of more tranches, however, the Fund was to impose increasingly severe conditions for the method and speed of balance-of-payments adjustment. Only when the deficit was considered to be fundamental by the Fund and the member country could a major devaluation be made.

Only with regard to portfolio and direct investment flows were international regulations conspicuously lacking. Yet these flows were much less important in the late 1940s than they are now. Thus in the postwar period international economic security did reach an acceptable level, mainly by separating trade and exchange-rate policies from foreign policy—making them into technical economic policy issues, subject to international scrutiny and some sanction power.

This is not to say that other approaches to international economic security are inconceivable or without influence. On the contrary, nations can limit their vulnerability by reducing economic openness or they can make international economic ties a function of their political and military relations. To a certain extent, these two alternatives have played a role in postwar developments.

The first one provided the impetus for including a series of escape clauses and exceptions in the GATT and creating its relatively weak multilateral surveillance system to evaluate unilateral trade restrictions. The desire to reduce economic openness also fostered attempts—led even by the United States in the case of voluntary export restraints—to circumvent the machinery of the GATT designed to limit market disruptions. In addition, the fear of openness was the source of the weak sanction power of the IMF, which delayed adjustment in surplus countries. The IMF had no way of imposing an acceleration of import growth, which would reduce their surplusses and also increase their economic openness. The desire to limit economic vulnerability is further evidenced by the absence of a powerful agreement on the liberalization of capital flows.

The second option, having economic ties follow military and political interests, was applied in the heavy reliance by Western European nations on the United States for their defense. Economically this implied the significant United States financial assistance to European recovery. However, once the GATT/IMF economic order was firmly established, these two alternative responses seemed to play only a secondary role.

Growth in economic openness and continuous decline in protectionism prevailed in the OECD economy for two decades. Tariff reductions, exchange rates, and financial facilities for central banks appeared to become issues of low politics because of the determination of the major economies to create and maintain an open world economic system. The world economy seemed to be governed by the rule of law, and both domestic and international politics appeared to recede into the background.

One crucial difference between national and international law, however, lies in the ultimate power of implementation and sanction. Since the late 1960s OECD countries have seen that international economic security is not found so much in subscription to global agreements, with procedures for multilateral surveillance, as in the presence of substantial diseconomies for countries that disobey or opt out. As argued by Hirsch and Doyle, diseconomies of that size are not always encountered by individual countries when they opt out. Because of the public-good character of the world economic order, a free rider can benefit without making a contribution or a commitment to the system. In the postwar system free riding was made very costly, however, as such a country would forgo financial "sweeteners" and political and military protection provided by a dominant power. Thus, underlying political and military security relations are a complementary set to functional international economic rules. So the *functional management* of economic relations among nations, favored by economists, is related to the *presence of power politics*, a fact typically ignored by economists. Therefore, the erosion of power configurations is not peripheral to the functioning of the economic order but rather has a pervasive impact on its operation. It follows that the search for international economic security is strongly linked to and even based on considerations of military security and international political relations.

If political relations are considered to be stable and reliable, they tend to form a foundation for intensive economic cooperation. Precisely because stability and reliability in Eastern Europe are based on Soviet hegemony, they have led to a substantial amount of economic cooperation through agreement on specialization and common enterprises. Among OECD countries the American security shield is the critical relationship for neutrals as well as NATO allies. In this context, it is interesting to note the surprising stability of bipolarity. The antagonism of the cold war, which minimized political and economic contacts between East and West, served as a catalyst to political, economic, and even cultural cooperation within the Eastern and Western spheres. This cooperation among allies added to perceptions of threat, furthered the arms race, and magnified the opposition between the two alliances. Meanwhile, at least a decade and a half passed with artificially tight security relations between the United States and its allies, Western Europe and Japan, making for stable and reliable economic relations.

The gradual erosion of the liberal economic order should not be attributed just to the replacement of bipolarity by multipolarity. Another aspect of the problem was that the group of countries whose political relations formed the basis for the economic order increasingly diverged in their international economic interests. For instance, the wave of new independent states significantly diminished developed-country control over raw-material supplies; the classic example is the rising importance of the OPEC countries. Also, trade contacts with Eastern Europe and some semi-industrialized countries began to increase the share of manufactured imports from outside the OECD group. In general, the OECD system grew more open, but virtually none of the outside countries adhered to the basic principles of the liberal economic order or were committed to the system through underlying political or security loyalties.

It follows from this analysis that the effort to exploit the benefits of international trade without reference to the political power configuration was bound to promote a decline in prices and supply stability for oil and raw materials. It was also sure to add to problems of market disruption that could no longer be solved under strict GATT procedures and lead to new but less reliable export markets. In this context, international economic security could be restored only by a series of measures such as ad hoc applications of voluntary export restraints, with all the political friction they create. Other measures include the reliance on bilateral trade regulation with, for example, ministers of industry and foreign relations selling technology and capital equipment to OPEC countries. Finally, and in a similar vein, governments pursued aggressive, state-sponsored export promotion. Such intervention is an approach that seeks to let domestic and international politics achieve the stability and reliability that have been lost with the frustration of the liberal economic system.

NATIONAL PROPENSITIES TO COOPERATE AMONG OECD STATES

Concern for international cooperation in economic affairs varies widely among the OECD countries. There are differences in attitude toward cooperation, differences of emphasis on particular issues, differences over both means and ends, and changes in the desire for cooperation over time. Only under specific circumstances or considerable pressure can all these differences be reconciled to form an effective world economic order. Thus expectations for future international economic cooperation should be only moderately optimistic. To clarify the origin and extent of these limitations on cooperation, a better understanding of why countries choose to cooperate is needed.

The desire to cooperate is shaped by a wide range of factors that can be organized into three groups: objective, functional, and governmental. First, the *objective* factors can be treated as constants here because they vary only in the long run. One such factor is the size of the country in terms of its area and population. Another is the basic level of economic development. In combination, these two determine the size of the market. Obviously, for a country the size of Belgium economic openness is far more important than for the United States. The position of Australia, despite its huge area, is far closer to that of Belgium than that of the United States.[4] Another determinant is the national endowment of natural resources, which encompasses everything from raw materials and fuel to access to the sea.

A second class of factors are *functional* in character. They concern the *efficiency gains* of international trade and invest-

[4]Both Australia and Belgium have slightly over 10 million inhabitants and comparable income levels; in square kilometers, Australia is about 270 times as large as Belgium.

ment, the added *stability* of living under a world monetary system, the *security gains* from the elimination of beggar-thy-neighbor policies, and the policy *consistency* provided by willingness to adjust national policies according to international negotiations. These advantages form the basis of the case for the international integration of markets. This means allowing economic subjects to freely determine what to purchase, where to produce, where to invest, and whether or not to migrate to work abroad. Theoretically world efficiency is enhanced to the benefit of everyone. These functional arguments are the crux of international economics and cannot possibly be dealt with here in their totality, but a few remarks should be made.

There is one paradox that is crucial to the understanding of international economic cooperation. It is believed that these functional benefits go to all parties participating in intensified international economic intercourse, but, nevertheless, many nations resist adopting a liberal approach to the world economy. There are a variety of explanations for this paradox, but two elements are of overriding importance as sources of resistance. The first one is that the objective of global economic efficiency must compete with other national objectives and aims, which, only when taken together, approximate national economic welfare. As noted before, the search for economic security at various levels illustrates this competition among objectives. The second element is that the conditions that market efficiency imposes or might eventually impose are deemed unacceptable in a growing number of situations.

Although OECD economies are still market-oriented, this resistance has led to a series of economic policies that call into question the size and, for practical purposes, even the existence of the functional gains. Of course, all nations perceive *some* benefits, and OECD nations have shown support for the liberal system as demonstrated by their growing economic openness. However, their adherence to a liberal world economic order is riddled with exceptions, conditionalities, and distortive practices, often without the deliberate intention of adversely affecting the international flow of trade and factors. Compared with the theoretical ideal of economists, the economic interaction among

ECONOMIC COOPERATION AMONG WESTERN COUNTRIES

states is a poor imitation that undermines both the generality and the clarity of the case for free trade and investment. The problem is further complicated by the fact that markets are distorted not only by government intervention but also by imperfections such as oligopolies, cartels, trade unions, and financial agglomerations. For example, the theoretical ideal does not take in intrafirm international trade, which has now grown to comprise about one-third of all international trade.[5] To what extent such intrafirm trade could properly be labeled an increase in world efficiency, given the possibilities for transfer pricing and other manipulations, seems impossible to answer. The multinational corporations also restrict trade by prohibiting certain exports of foreign subsidiaries, through market-sharing arrangements and other means that largely remain invisible.

The host of governmental and private deviations from the competitive free market ideal cause pressures on governments to even out domestic or foreign distortions through redistributive policies, which in turn tend to politicize economic issues. The United States promotes exports by allowing firms to erect formal subsidiaries that can claim favorable tax treatment if they export 95 percent of their "sales." Such policies are surely not in tune with the liberal model and cause political concern among those competing with the United States. Another example is the unjustified irritation in the United States about the restitution of the value-added tax to European Community (EC) firms for exports. Although this is an intricate issue, its redistributive potential is clear if one realizes that the value-added tax in the EC is much higher than the not fully comparable sales tax in the United States. All in all, the functional benefits, which are shared

[5]This is a guess, as there are no adequate figures on *all* intrafirm international trade for *all* multinational corporations. Only figures relating to the United States are fairly adequate. In 1975 affiliate exports to the United States accounted for 32 percent of total United States imports, compared with 25 percent in 1966 (*Survey of Current Business*, February 1977, p. 34). However, another 4 to 5 percent of United States imports is accounted for by wholesale affiliate imports of Western European multinationals in the United States from their overseas parent companies and an even higher figure holds for Japanese affiliates in the United States (*Survey of Current Business*, May 1976; figure for 1974).

by everyone, do motivate nations to cooperate. But this "functional logic" should be treated with utmost care in a world economy riddled with inconsistencies that frustrate its success.

A third group of factors are *governmental*. To functionalist thinkers governments are a nuisance at best and usually a grave source of conflict. For them, nations should be motivated to cooperate solely by the benefits derived from the unrestricted international mobility of goods and productive factors. Thus, in their terms, interventionist governments, by their attempts to control markets, inherently reduce effective cooperation. This position, however, mistakenly assumes that theory provides a faithful image of reality. It is based on a model that neglects many of the problems that pluralist democratic countries with mixed economies are bound to face. It assumes perfect competition, the general availability of knowledge and technology, and instantaneous adjustments, including downward wage and price flexibility. It takes as given the objective of output maximization and the underlying income distribution, expecting all individuals to strive for private income maximization. But this excludes other behavior, such as seeking security from the vagaries of world competition or attempting by political means to change some basic conditions in this harsh and peculiar economy. Needless to say, governments produce policies on all of these difficult points, either because of the demands of constituency and electoral politics or in reaction to market imperfections such as oligopolies, cartels, and trade unions.

The role of governmental factors in motivating nations to cooperate in the world economy is clearest in the context of the broad aims of the Western nation-state. For example, cooperative attitudes are partially a function of international security linkages, which create world power structures and set the tone of foreign policies. National security also tends to impose certain limits on economic openness in agriculture, arms production, energy, and some other sectors. Feelings of independence or economic nationalism may limit openness even further. The crucial question here is, if citizens derive satisfaction from a mild xenophobia, on what grounds can it be condemned? In a democratic country, people can openly dislike the fact that foreigners have a large stake in production, investment, and distribution; thus marginal or even discrete alterations in the economy, resulting from the preferences of the majority, should be accepted.

Rather than give more examples like the one above, I believe it is useful now to return to the functional issues and review them in the light of government behavior. One principal advantage of the liberal system consists in the benefits of a unified world monetary system, compared by Professor Kindleberger with the benefits of one world language. The current flexibility of exchange rates proves that national propensities to cooperate in the monetary sphere are relatively low. In the EC, ambitious plans for a common currency have foundered on the rocks of national unwillingness to surrender control over currency. Curiously enough, a major incentive behind EC attempts to create one money is precisely because it represents one aspect of "nationhood." However, there are also economic reasons for the refusal to give up national currencies. One world money or its functional equivalent, fixed exchange rates, would limit the freedom of governments in economic policy. Although the freedom created by flexibility seems less than expected,[6] it does relieve some of the pressure from the general economic policy overload and is therefore welcomed. In addition, flexibility acts as an ultimate buffer against economic shocks from outside the country that can hurt the domestic economy and reduce politicians' chances of getting reelected.

The security of knowing that other nations will not apply beggar-thy-neighbor policies has obvious functional benefits, but these become much more complex in the light of governmental factors. Here, we get a good look at the beast called "cooperation." The sensitivity of national economic policies to international economic processes produces different reactions, depending on whether economic policies are mutually supporting or conflicting. Policy *effectiveness* is helped by mutually supporting policies and hurt by conflicting ones.

[6]For a good, albeit brief, discussion on the insulative effects of exchange-rate flexibility, see Marina v. N. Whitman, "Sustaining the International Economic System: Issues for U.S. Policy," *Essays in International Finance*, no. 121, Princeton University, Princeton, N.J., 1977, pp. 21–22.

In general there are three possible policy reactions: a return to laissez faire that reduces policy intervention, the unilateral limitation of economic openness, or the international agreement not to apply conflicting policy instruments. The first policy reaction, while sometimes advocated, can be disregarded because it is made irrelevant by the wide scope and political importance of economic policy in OECD economies.

The second solution, the unilateral limitation of economic openness, is controversial in that it gives short-term relief at the risk of retaliatory reactions from other countries. Since successful short-run policy achievements can at times be quite appealing, the unilateral use of tariff barriers or deliberate depreciation cannot be dismissed as entirely irrational. After all, a substantial loss of policy effectiveness is a *threat* to a government's ability to follow policies that will sustain its commitments to voters. Loss of control over their economies leaves nations at the mercy of international developments, and this is precisely what they find difficult to accept because they are expected to provide and maintain domestic economic security. They are in a double bind because attempts to guarantee domestic and individual economic security increasingly threaten international economic security and attempts to promote the liberal economic order threaten the effectiveness of national economic policy instruments.

This dilemma is illustrated by the case for using beggar-thy-neighbor policy instruments, which hinges on two political judgments that destabilize international economic relations. These are that short-run, or sectoral, political interests should have priority over the benefits of international commerce and that retaliation is not expected to occur. It is particularly over these decisions that *economic* policy dilemmas become *politicized* and *domestic* issues become *internationalized*. The mere consideration of such a strategy can produce political strains in a heavily interdependent system.

One way to avoid this problem is to take the third route, that is, contain conflicting instruments of international economic policy through agreements that leave the supporting instruments of domestic policy at the discretion of national policy makers. To some degree, OECD members, with the leadership of the United States, have done this because of a common fear of a return to the protectionism of the 1930s.[7] However, this cooperation was negative; countries were buying off some of the beggar-thy-neighbor policies but leaving enough autonomy, loopholes, and escape clauses to allow the agreements to be accepted at home. This has been the basis of almost all international economic cooperation in the postwar period.

This negative loyalty is most fragile because *every government's acceptance of its reduced autonomy depends on other countries being willing to do the same*. The current international economic system is therefore based on confidence, regular consultation, and continuous sensitivity to any use of beggar-thy-neighbor policies in the system. Its stability is always threatened by the effects of external shocks, deteriorating policy performance, or general economic recessions, all of which make protective policies attractive.

The security gains from the mutual surrendering of autonomy, which can be termed "negative cooperation," are therefore substantial but necessarily conditional. Feeling relatively secure because of the high level of this policy cooperation, OECD member governments have taken an increasingly favorable attitude to economic openness, that is, they can afford to let the functional arguments for free trade prevail. Economic growth has added to this conviction, as adjustment to greater openness can take place easily in a favorable environment. Today, the future of this security is in doubt because the maintenance of economic openness requires enforced market adjustment to regional and sectoral shifts leading to unemployment in a low-growth climate. Eventual domestic resistance to such conditions threatens to provoke a decline in economic openness.

A third functional benefit that also depends on government

[7]Since the focus is on (individual) governmental behavior, this remark neglects the conditions for successful leadership and the difficulties in persuading potential free riders to join by making opting out very unattractive in military and financial terms. See Hirsh and Doyle, op. cit. Clearly, such effective leadership will duly increase other countries' propensities to cooperate in the world economy.

behavior is the policy consistency achieved by the willingness of countries to adjust national policies through international negotiations. The policies referred to here do not conflict outright, as with tariffs or export quotas, but instead are usually directed at influencing the overall level of expenditure and prices in the domestic economy (as opposed to influencing the composition of expenditure and relative prices). The government's willingness to adjust these policies for international cooperation is inhibited by domestic concerns. Strong political pressure from below is created by electoral and constituency politics, and politicians are often more responsive to these domestic concerns because of their desire to remain in power. Even countries with open economies have upheld an obstinate preference to stay at least in potential control of their fate. However, the suppression of beggar-thy-neighbor policies has reduced the ability of governments to insulate themselves despite their growing policy ambitions. In response to this limitation there has been a trend toward more delicate domestic political compromises on economic policy. These in turn are so intricate that they do not have the flexibility necessary for international negotiation. Another consequence has been the introduction of a wave of specific domestic policies that have secondary effects, which serve as a partial substitute for the inapplicable beggar-thy-neighbor instruments. Examples are regional and sectoral aids, industrial policies, government procurement policies, adjustment assistance programs, and employment subsidies.[8] These policies are an added burden to national budgets, and they further increase the complexity and sensitivity of negotiations for policy consistency.

In conclusion, the propensity of nations to cooperate in the world economy is determined by many complex processes. Cooper's classic and succinct formulation integrates most of the aforementioned elements. He sees "the central problem of international economic cooperation" as "how to keep the manifold benefits of extensive international economic intercourse free of

---

[8]Of course, the move to exchange-rate flexibility has also contributed significantly to relieving the pressures for applying beggar-thy-neighbor policies despite its macroeconomic character.

crippling restrictions while at the same time preserving a maximum degree of freedom for each nation to pursue its legitimate economic objectives."[9] Although this formulation does not refer to the higher aims of nations and fails to encompass the cooperative adaptation of national policies or the issue of a world money, it does bring out the basic tension between governmental policies and international markets without condemning intervention as dysfunctional and irrational. On the contrary, the political legitimacy of economic policy making in democracies is emphasized.

[9]Richard Cooper, *The Economic of Interdependence*, McGraw-Hill for the Council on Foreign Relations, New York, 1968, p. 5.

TWO

The Nature of International Economic Cooperation

NEGATIVE AND POSITIVE POLICY COOPERATION

An inquiry into the properties of cooperation is impeded by the absence of a common, well-accepted methodology. In economic theory, there is a great discrepancy between the sophisticated analysis of international markets and the scanty treatment of the internationalization of policy. The theory of global and regional commodity-market integration, as well as its distortions, has been thoroughly developed, while the theory of international economic policy cooperation has been all but neglected except for discussion of the elimination of border interventions.

Cooperation may be understood as any common action aimed at improving a working system. This definition tells us very little, as many kinds, forms, and intensities of cooperation can be imagined. For clarity the term needs further specification. But part of its political—as opposed to analytical—appeal lies in this vagueness: it can provide a common denominator for unifying negotiating parties.

Using the principle of national sovereignty as the cutting edge, I divide policy cooperation into *negative* and *positive* forms. Negative cooperation involves removing discriminatory treatment against goods and factor flows from abroad. Positive cooperation is the construction of institutions and agreements for *common* policy making. The major difference between the two forms is that negative policy cooperation merely limits policy autonomy *without* transferring jurisdiction, but positive policy cooperation *encroaches on domestic jurisdiction.*

As nearly all OECD economies arose from the liberal nation-states of the nineteenth century, it is no wonder that negative policy cooperation has been emphasized most. Negative cooperation leads to economic openness, which in turn tends to integrate markets, leading to a convergence of prices, wages, and interest rates in the participating countries. The approximation of one OECD market for the various commodities and services and the narrowing of factor costs among trading partners have traditionally been offered as evidence that the optimal division of labor has been enhanced. Since it is in the interest of all nations to obtain maximum production from the world's resources, the case for negative cooperation is a strong one indeed.

The aim of negative policy cooperation is to suppress conflicting policy instruments, in particular tariff barriers and other forms of protection. National policy autonomy is substantially reduced, but recourse to protection will usually remain possible in emergencies. In well-developed trade systems this recourse is under multilateral surveillance. The intensity of negative policy cooperation is indicated by how much multilateral decision making exists in the acknowledgment of emergencies and the choice of protective instruments. A country's sensitivity to these multilateral decisions increases the more concerned it is with its ability to choose policy instruments. Hence, negative policy integration not only leads to market integration but also increases policy interdependence.

In OECD economies this growth of policy interdependence generates political concern because it makes domestic decision making harder. Protection, for instance, through tariffs on imports, gives governments added control over the patterns of domestic spending which helps prevent, soften, or postpone the use of policies that can control spending on the aggregate level only through fiscal and monetary instruments. The policies at the aggregate level are less discrete and often more painful to the domestic economy in the short run than the acceptance of protection and a more closed economy. This situation also has international implications because, with the gradual loss of protective instruments through negative cooperation, governments are not only forced to control spending at the aggregate level but they are also more directly influenced by economic expansion and contraction among their most significant trading partners. Thus policy interdependence generates both domestic and international political concern.

OECD governments recognize the inevitability of negative policy cooperation, but their loyalty to it is not absolute. This is the source of the major problem with negative policy cooperation. Loopholes, escape clauses, and the possibility of substituting domestic policies for border protection measures all frustrate the integration of economies. These are internal manifestations of the search for national economic security which attempt to avoid upsetting the delicate stability of the liberal economic order without, however, accepting its ultimate domestic consequences.

Positive cooperation is much harder to achieve for both political and economic reasons. The political unwillingness to engage in common international policy making has its origins in the success of national political, economic, and cultural integration. National integration directs the loyalty, concerns, and political activities of citizens toward the nation. Politicians in turn further confirm and respond to this national loyalty. Given this environment, they are wary of transferring their control to intergovernmental or supranational authorities because they will then lose a potential means of satisfying national preferences. In addition, positive cooperation in major issue areas is likely to be so sensitive in domestic politics that it could become an electoral issue with tremendous emotional impact on the nation.

Economic resistance can be traced back to the allegiance to free markets and fears for international *dirigisme*. Conflicting national views on how to solve economic policy dilemmas also add to this resistance. These economic disputes are rarely either theoretical or technical; instead they usually conceal conflicting international preferences over the pattern and speed of achieving adjustment.

NEGATIVE ECONOMIC COOPERATION IN THE CONTEXT OF TRADITIONAL FOREIGN ECONOMIC POLICY

Postwar negative economic cooperation has been based on certain implicit conceptions about economic policy. Three basic categories of economic policies can be distinguished: foreign, demand management, and specific domestic economic policies.

Foreign economic policy consists of trade policy, exchange-rate policy, and other international controls on goods and money flows. All these instruments are *expenditure-switching* policies, that is, they induce a shift of domestic expenditure away from or toward foreign goods. Therefore, foreign economic policy can directly damage the performance of other economies, implying that all its elements are the concern of other states and are issues of international cooperation.

Demand management policies consist of monetary (manipulation of the interest rate and the money supply), fiscal, and budgetary policy. In the postwar period these policies were *not* considered to be directly subject to international cooperation because it was generally thought that exclusive reliance on these instruments for adjustment would not produce the beggar-thy-neighbor effects created by expenditure-switching devices. General domestic policies are concerned with the *expenditure level* in the economy. In the case of downward adjustment, the hardships of national expenditure reduction fall primarily on the country itself. In such a case the resulting reduction of imports is accepted as an inevitable part of adjustment. If general domestic policies cause an increase in the level of expenditure, the impact is internationally reinforcing because some of the additional expenditure will go to foreign goods. These considerations are correct given the underlying model, which assumes fixed exchange rates and the absence of capital mobility, two assumptions that were reasonably approximated in the 1950s and early 1960s but are anachronistic today.

Specific domestic measures consist of a large series of other policies and regulations that were assumed to have no systematic international effects. They include business and tax laws; social security transfers; and the regulation of specific sectors, such as transport, gas, water and electricity, health and safety require-ments, government procurement, and others. The absence of direct systematic international repercussions made them unin-teresting for international cooperation, regardless of the fact that they were integral to the various national economies. Their in-direct importance was recognized in part by the International Trade Organization (ITO) but not pursued in the GATT. In the Havana Charter that laid the basis for the ITO, internal revenue duties on coffee, tobacco, and hard liquor were treated as similar in effect to tariffs, but this was not so in the GATT. The Haberler Report concludes "As internal taxes are not at the present time deemed to be negotiable in the same way as ordinary customs duties, a number of importing countries have declined to enter into negotiations for the reduction of revenue."[10]

In the light of this analysis we can see that in the postwar period expenditure-switching policies were considered to be in-ternationally conflictual and therefore subject to negative co-operation. Expenditure-level policies, on the other hand, were considered to be internationally reinforcing or at least as not to shift the burden of adjustment to other countries, thus making international cooperation unnecessary in this sphere. Specific domestic policies were thought to be irrelevant to cooperation for all practical purposes. One advantage of this division is that it defines a sphere for cooperation. In addition, the elements of the sphere are all similar instruments; in principle they can all be *removed* without an elaborate common policy structure en-croaching on domestic jurisdiction.

Postwar Achievements

Since 1945 a remarkable number of international organizations have attempted to improve economic cooperation. If we limit ourselves to Western industrialized countries, the most effective organizations have been the GATT and IMF (dominated by rich

---

[10]GATT, *Trends in International Trade* (Haberler Report), Geneva, 1958, p. 107. Quoted from Jacques Polak, "International Coordination of Economic Policy," *IMF Staff Papers*, July 1962, p. 165.

countries but universal in membership); the OECD; and such regional economic organizations as Benelux, the EC, and the European Free Trade Association (EFTA). Negative economic cooperation has been their central concern.

The GATT has been a politicized affair right from the start. The tension between functional and governmental factors is immediately apparent when one analyzes the agreement. Following the Curzons, the GATT can be said to have four pillars.[11]

First, its emphasis is on nondiscrimination in trade policies. This principle is designed to depoliticize trade relations by prohibiting bilateralism and preferential trading clubs that exclude benefits to third parties. Trade discrimination fits beautifully into the high politics of spheres of influence, and it is also part of the selective granting of favors to friendly countries. It definitely contributed to the mismanagement of the world economy in the interwar period and thus to World War II. After the war trade discrimination was still a strong force. Great Britain would accept nondiscrimination only after the exemption of its own Preferential Scheme with the Commonwealth. The United States, recognizing the political significance of a strong Western Europe in the cold war, pushed for Article XXIV of the GATT, exempting customs unions and free trade areas from the principle. Eventually, this facilitated the formation of the EC and EFTA. Thus, the practical barriers to depoliticization were so strong that the United States was the only industrialized country that was always discriminated *against*.

Second, there was the principle of trade barrier reduction, and third, the concept of reciprocity as the means for negotiating the reductions. Reciprocal trade liberalization through multilateral negotiations, or "rounds," has been highly successful. However, it is interesting to note that reciprocity is prescribed only in Article XXVIII of the agreement and that trade liberalization has gained importance only as a result of the same article. The rising importance of trade liberalization is largely explained by the

[11]Gerald Curzon and Victoria Curzon, "The Management of Trade Relations in the GATT," in Andrew Shonfield (ed.), *International Economic Relations of the Western World 1959–71*, vol. 1, published for the Royal Institute of International Affairs by Oxford University Press, London, 1976.

leadership of the United States and the advantageous environment provided by economic growth. The requirement of reciprocity is largely explained by Keynesian fears of a painful national adjustment to lower protection. In an economy with downward wage rigidity and barely sufficient effective demand, unilateral tariff concessions will decrease demand for domestic products, causing unemployment. Reciprocity provides a clear basis for constituency politics by creating pressure for trade liberalization in the export sector, where tariff concessions of other countries will induce a boom, neutralizing the negative employment effect. Reciprocity also fits in with the diplomatic objective to conclude an equivalent exchange of concessions.

Fourth, for the first time in history, an international trade order was established. The most important elements of that order were that trade barriers could be increased only by invoking escape clauses and that import restrictions such as quotas had to be dismantled. In addition, a framework for nondiscriminatory tariff reduction was constructed, with the initiative for reductions left in the hands of participants, and escape clauses could be implemented only under multilateral surveillance through detailed procedures with an ultimate sanction of common retaliation. Escape clauses were rarely invoked[12] and were often deliberately avoided. According to the GATT, if tariff concessions do induce massive imports and cause "serious injury," Article XIX can be invoked for "emergency action." The fact that this clause has been avoided conceals a complex and growing network of voluntary export restraints, informally imposed by agreements outside the strict GATT framework. These informal agreements illustrate the ingenious ways in which governments keep their behavior consistent with the rule of international trade law without accepting the domestic political consequences.

This view of a politicized trade diplomacy seems to contradict the notion that matters of international trade kept a low political profile in the 1950s and 1960s. Or, to use Cooper's apt phrase, international relations in the Western world worked on a "two track system," where trade policy and foreign policy were kept

[12]Ibid., p. 162.

on separate tracks that were not supposed to cross.[13] The contradiction largely disappears if one understands the politicization of international trade relations not just in terms of the high politics of traditional foreign policy but also as the links between domestic politics and trade policy. As mentioned in Chapter 1, domestic politics can deprive trade policy of its functional orientation just as much as can a formal link between foreign policy and trade policy.

Experience with the GATT demonstrates that domestic politics, in particular the search for various forms of economic security, have greatly influenced trade diplomacy. But this does not invalidate Cooper's basic point. The politicization was successfully contained within the sphere of trade policy and was not permitted to spill over to other areas of foreign policy. It is, however, important to realize that some vital foreign policy conditions, such as a reliable and stable security system and the leadership of the United States, were essential to the effectiveness of this separation.

In general the limited politicization of trade policy has not proved to be too great a barrier to the unprecedented success of trade liberalization. Without going into specifics, it is probably fair to say that the principle of reciprocity, the gradual nature of the liberalization process, and the widespread prevalence of economic growth made it possible, especially for the European countries, to respond positively to a series of American initiatives. This development has now created a level of economic interdependence that has increased every country's stake in the maintenance of the system. This is perhaps the greatest achievement of negative trade cooperation. It has generated its own perpetuation by making the cost of opting out close to prohibitive.

Monetary cooperation in the IMF was much less politicized, or so it seemed. The impression that the problems of the international monetary system were primarily technical and could be discussed in a functional setting is quite understandable. The basic elements of trade policy are easy to grasp and of direct interest to many segments of business and labor, but the mon-

[13]Richard Cooper, "Trade Policy Is Foreign Policy," in Richard Cooper (ed.), *A Reordered World*, Potomac Association, Washington, D.C., 1973.

etary system operates at a higher level of theoretical complexity and produces only global effects, rather than sectoral ones, making it of more peripheral interest to the business community. Moreover, monetary affairs are rarely politicized even domestically. Many OECD countries have relatively independent central banks, and their presidents tend to avoid political life.

Nevertheless, two major forms of politicization have played an important role in the IMF system. These are the political preferences implicit in the rules adopted at Bretton Woods in 1944 and the political salience of crisis management in the 1960s. On balance, this politicization stretched the life of the Bretton Woods system and fostered negative monetary cooperation.

The strict legal version of the Bretton Woods system differed from the way the system actually functioned. The rules combined elements of three ideals: the gold standard, a world bank, and flexible exchange rates. The first ideal was partially incorporated by the emphasis on stable exchange rates: the pegged rate was to be changed only when a "fundamental disequilibrium" in the balance of payments arose.[14] The gold standard was also reflected in multilateral convertibility and the link between currency and gold. The United States, in its leadership role, voluntarily offered gold convertibility for the dollar. This kind of pegged system, like the gold standard, can work only if balance-of-payments adjustment is accepted symmetrically by surplus and deficit countries. But the automatism of the gold standard was no longer acceptable in the domestic politics of the participating countries. They could not tolerate having gold and foreign-exchange reserves determine domestic money supply. Thus, adjustment by surplus countries was not certain. They could accumulate foreign exchange without serious pressures, but deficit countries, by contrast, would see their international liquidity dry up if they avoided adjustment.[15] This practice caused some fear of a deflationary bias in the system.

[14]Small changes could be made without the Fund's approval (only its consultation) and without a fundamental disequilibrium.

[15]Technically this could be prevented by the "scarce currency" clause, a sort of multilateral punishment of the surplus country. However, as the dollar was scarce for over 10 years, for quite different reasons, the clause was frozen. That precedent blocked its later use.

Another difference with the gold standard is the domestic political concern with the *speed* of adjustment. It is here that the ideal of a world central bank appears in a limited way. To slow the speed of adjustment and smooth the process, credit facilities were devised. A deficit country could thus draw credit tranches from the Fund to handle its adjustment deficits, every tranche being one-fourth of its quota.[16] The IMF was to impose ever more severe conditions regarding domestic adjustment policies when more credit tranches were demanded. In this way the IMF functioned as a sort of bank of central banks. This instrument of conditional finance in the hands of a global institution is an excellent example of *positive* cooperation and, in the formal sense, quite an achievement. In practice, the facility was rarely used, except by some poor or semi-industrialized countries. Rich countries with hard currencies seemed to find the procedure politically humiliating. Their avoidance of positive monetary cooperation through the Fund influenced the nature of international monetary relations profoundly, especially in the period 1960–1973.

After the European and Japanese economic recoveries, the United States began to experience balance-of-payments deficits. Initially no one in the United States government considered drawing from the Fund, in view of the large United States gold stocks. After some time, however, the gold stock had diminished and American short-term liabilities had grown rapidly, indicating that the United States would have to adjust. Since United States emphasis on adjustment had clearly colored the IMF rules, impartial observers might have expected prompt action from the Americans. The United States, however, did not adjust, and other countries accepted this fact, which teaches us a lot about the interaction of politics and economics in postwar monetary cooperation.

First, it should be noted that theoretically it would have been quite easy for the United States to adjust at the end of the 1950s. The Americans would merely have had to limit autonomous (i.e.,

---

[16]As quotas were in some way related to the country's economic openness and financial strength, the tranches were related to expected needs. The total number of tranches for each member was at first 5 and later 8.

not market-determined) transfers, such as development aid and military aid, over the capital account because its trade balance was still in surplus. Most countries fear adjustment, as they usually must alter their trade balance instead of their capital account. This means limiting national spending, which is usually politically unpopular at home. But for the United States, the political and military leader of the West, the transfers on the capital account were instruments of political and strategic foreign policy and thus not easily manipulated. In addition, very few foreign politicians complained, because expenditures on United States troops abroad, arms purchases, and aid to poor countries helped relieve balance-of-payments pressures in Western Europe and Japan. They knew that the United States deficit was a boon for them because it permitted a higher growth rate without external imbalance, thus enhancing their political popularity at home.

President de Gaulle was an exception. Being more mercantilist, France cheerfully enjoyed external surplusses and also used the earned dollars to challenge United States leadership—a typical manifestation of high politics. De Gaulle's main objection was that the United States was able to print dollars for foreigners at zero cost and obtain a net inflow of benefits in return. The profits from this are called *seignorage*. In challenging American leadership, de Gaulle purposefully ignored the cost of the United States nuclear capacity or the balance-of-payments benefits that went to the Europeans and instead concentrated on the privilege of seignorage.

The United States deficits were also informally welcomed because they created a much needed source of international liquidity. The growth of the world stock of nonprivate gold was lagging far behind the growth of international transactions, and this discrepancy fed fears that all countries would start to scramble for gold, producing mercantilist havoc in the world economy. The United States deficits solved the world liquidity problem, but they also seemed to create new troubles for the monetary system. As Triffin first argued, ultimately confidence in the dollar disappears as United States liabilities pile up. The first gold/dollar crisis occurred in 1960, and several were to follow.

The initial reaction of the hard currency countries was *not* to

107

strengthen positive cooperation by asking the IMF to apply its rules strictly or by creating a world money to parallel national currencies and be issued by the IMF. Instead, ad hoc finance facilities were agreed to in the so-called Group of Ten, swap arrangements were constructed, and Roosa bonds were invented, but fundamental solutions were postponed. The incentives to cooperate were high, and recurring crises in the system added to the intensity and multitude of cooperation efforts, despite de Gaulle's ostentatious gold conversions. Cooperation became more politicized, however, as German support for the dollar was linked explicitly to the security issue of American troops in the Federal Republic. Problems arose *among* Western Europeans due to differences in inflation rates and economic growth. In 1964 Italy and Great Britain were aided by ad hoc financing, but in 1967 the pound was devalued. In 1968 the United States and France pressured Bonn to raise the value of the mark, but it refused, and in 1969 the French franc devalued and the Deutsche mark finally revalued.

Decisions about parity changes seemed to be linked to high politics through a sense of national pride and economic strength that made changes in the exchange rate bad for a country's self-image. This situation produced a common interest in facilities that would stabilize the system, for example, by creating a nonpolitical source of liquidity: the special drawing right (SDR). The idea was to eventually replace all dollars being used as reserves with SDRs that would then operate as a world money among central banks. But here, too, practice eroded an important piece of positive cooperation. United States deficits in 1970 and 1971 swamped the world with dollars, and as a result confidence in the system was about to disappear before any new institutions could be set in place.

The third ideal of the Bretton Woods system was flexibility of exchange rates. It is generally accepted that adjustment is not automatic and that the speed of adjustment is a legitimate political concern. For any monetary system to work, *some* flexibility has to be accepted. For many years, pegged exchange rates were perceived as fixed under a gold standard. After the mid-sixties, when rates were altered more regularly, it was still thought that the dollar exchange rate was unmovable. It was recognized by the late 1960s that the United States finally had to do something drastic about its incredible deficits. A United States devaluation was ruled out because the immediate devaluation of all other currencies was expected to follow. This implies that the overvaluation of the dollar was a product of the search for export surplusses by other countries. This search can be explained only by the beneficial employment effects created by a trade surplus. Once again, it appears that domestic political preferences, fed by Keynesian policy perspectives, were an important undercurrent of monetary tensions.

Views of flexibility underwent great changes after the West Germans let the Deutsche mark float for the first time, in September 1969, before pegging it anew. In 1970 even the IMF itself started to reconsider its position. Without going into the details of the money muddle in the period from 1969 until 1976,[17] there is some merit in contrasting present flexibility with the philosophy about flexibility in the Bretton Woods system. In fact, flexibility was accepted as a necessary evil for major adjustments, but it was to be contained as much as possible. This rigid position came from a common fear of the competitive devaluations that plagued the thirties. Flexibility was limited to the exceptional case of a "fundamental" disequilibrium in the balance of payments, determined through consultation with the Fund.

Now, with floating exchange rates, flexibility is continuous and therefore not subject to special cases. Since 1976, the rules explicitly recognize complete flexibility of exchange rates. If the rates are well managed by the various central banks, flexibility should not lead to competitive devaluations. It is this question of competitive devaluations that has survived as the crucial issue in negative monetary cooperation. Flexibility has surely depoliticized international monetary affairs. Exchange rates are no longer defended on silly grounds of "grandeur" or fear of electoral defeat. In addition, flexibility has greatly reduced potential

[17]In 1976 the IMF rules were changed on the basis of the Jamaica Agreement. See *IMF Survey*, January 19, 1976. For a detailed account of the recent monetary history, see Robert Solomon, *The International Monetary System 1945–1976: An Insiders View*, Harper and Row, New York, 1977.

tensions among OECD economies, in the face of varied rates of inflation, large oil bills, and differing capacities to pay for this oil. In an interdependent economic group such as the OECD, there is simply no realistic alternative to flexible exchange rates under present circumstances. It is naïve and illusionary to expect that all the individual financial adjustments among OECD countries and the overall adjustment toward OPEC countries can be dealt with by a multilateral agreement.

Negative cooperation was also fostered by the Organization for European Economic Cooperation (OEEC) and its institutional successor, the OECD. The OEEC was a group of Western European nations that controlled the allocation of American Marshall Plan aid. It was explicitly formed for all-European economic cooperation, and it was probably the most effective instrument of American leadership in the economic system. GATT's trade liberalization was helped tremendously by the ambitious OEEC liberalization program of the 1950s. In the wake of this enthusiasm, the OEEC sponsored negotiations for an all-European free trade area (excluding Eastern Europe) in the Maudling Committee. But in this case, the United States thought that the EEC would be more effective in creating a strong partner. As a result, Maudling failed and the EEC and EFTA were founded.[18]

After 1960, with the establishment of the European trade areas and the end of the recovery, the United States, Japan, and other industrial states became members and the OEEC was changed to the OECD. The organization was thus transformed into the "high-level, low-key"[19] cooperation center for the wealthy countries of the world. The philosophy of a liberal international economic order was explicitly laid out in its codes on the liberalization of capital flows and invisible trade. Together with the long-functioning code for commodity trade, the OECD codes reflect a nearly ideal vision of negative economic cooperation.

[18]On July 1, 1977, however, the all-European free trade area came into being for industrial products.

[19]Miriam Camps, "First World Relationships: The Role of the OECD," *Council Papers on International Affairs*, no. 5, Council on Foreign Relations, New York, 1975.

Behind the scenes, the Working Parties of its Economic Policy Committee went even further, by attempting secret and informal efforts toward cooperation. Especially Working Party III played a role in crisis management in the monetary sphere and in the depoliticization of parity changes through secret discussions.

In the mid-1970s, the OECD has also been used by the United States as a vehicle to further cooperation among developed market economies. Since 1974, "trade pledges" have been made by joint ministerial sessions, the International Energy Agency was erected, substantial facilities were created in the Financial Support Fund, and a code about multinationals was agreed to by the members. In addition, the OECD is very active in sponsoring common statements, conferences, and publications about economic problems facing the members, such as the McCracken Report on the appropriate strategy to decelerate inflation without increasing unemployment or damaging negative cooperation.

The OECD is a powerless organization in institutional terms, but to conclude that it is therefore of marginal importance is wrong. The OECD is not merely a source of reliable statistics or an impartial think tank. In a sense, the OECD is the only major international economic organization that purposefully strives for a completely liberal economic order. In times of prolonged stagnation, the need for a staunch, international defender of functional policy cooperation is great. An active OECD creates a spirit that makes it harder for governments to enact selfish economic policies.

Limitations of Negative Cooperation

The clarity of the implicit division of economic policy into three areas—foreign, demand management, and specific domestic—has gradually faded away. One reason has been the increasing sensitivity of governments to the international impact of demand management and specific domestic policies, given the current level of economic interdependence. The impression is that especially the specific domestic policies have served as substitutes for tariffs or other expenditure switching policies. Another reason for this loss of clarity has been the failure of negative cooperation to cover important aspects of international commerce. In the traditional conception of foreign economic policy, both portfolio and direct investment flows are conspicuously lacking.

To illustrate the problems created, two examples are provided. The first concerns the supposed substitution of tariffs with non-tariff distortions (NTDs). Only two NTDs, quotas and licensing schemes, were dealt with in the GATT although vague references to other barriers were also made. Obviously domestic biases in government spending, regional and sectoral aids, customs valuation traditions,[20] nationalized industries, research and development subsidies, and tied development aid will induce a composition and magnitude of international trade that are surely far from what is theoretically optimal. These programs reflect national preoccupations with the level and the quality of employment, the distribution of income between sectors and regions, the possession of technology, and the desire to provide development aid.

To an extent that is very hard to determine, these *specific domestic* policies have expenditure-switching effects and may be considered substitutes for tariffs. The fact that these policies are ostensibly domestic but have international impacts blurs distinctions and creates a formidable negotiation problem. It is theoretically possible to conduct negative cooperation for some instruments, i.e., forbid biases in government spending or prohibit tying aid. However, governments are not likely to be willing to give up so much control, because these substitutes for tariffs have made it easier for them to accept trade liberalization and the elimination of them will deprive governments of instruments to soften adjustment. The limitation of some NTDs also touches on delicate political issues, such as nationalized industries, and can lead to a detailed intrusion into national policies on direct and indirect taxation or on health and safety requirements. In short, some policies are simply not negotiable, other ones do involve negative cooperation but with tremendous obstacles to

[20]This term refers to the way national governments value goods and subject them to tariffs. Governmental biases in the application of tariffs can create distortions in trade.

obtaining reciprocity, and still others require positive policy cooperation because they cannot be removed for political reasons.

The second example concerns international direct investment. The hot money flows of the 1930s and the relative insignificance of international direct investment before about 1960 were the reasons international capital flows were seen as a secondary item. The urge for free international trade was not echoed by a movement toward one international capital market. No attempt was made at removing restrictions from exchange and stock markets or from international banking. Therefore, the flourishing of international banking on the Euro-currency and the Euro-bond market is quite amazing. Likewise, in the area of international direct investment, cooperation was entirely lacking, but in this case anarchy has been the result.

Initially the Keynesian view that foreign direct investment inflows increase effective demand along with structural enlargement of productive capacity[21] made a case for a liberal international investment policy. This position was strengthened by the great differences in technology among OECD countries and the belief that liberalization would close technological gaps. Furthermore, a liberal policy complemented the economic philosophy that led to the elaborate work on negative cooperation in trade, so at first there were few restrictions on foreign direct investment.

The reality of the 1960s increasingly moved away from the liberal vision. The Netherlands and West Germany had *liberal* policies on both inflows and outflows of direct investment. France, however, attempted to *restrict* foreign inflows by various means, sometimes even by direct orders from President de Gaulle. Belgium pursued a fairly aggressive policy to *promote* foreign direct investment. In many countries research about the growth of foreign-controlled economic activity led to a reappraisal of liberal inflow policies. In the United States, fears of Japanese and Arabian ''takeovers'' led to a large-scale investigation in 1974, but to only marginal new legislation in 1976. However, the United States did (and the United Kingdom still

[21]If they do not substitute for intended investments by nationals.

does) *restrict* outflows of direct investment in an attempt to decrease balance-of-payments deficits.

Japan, on the other hand, *encouraged* such outflows between 1971 and 1974 in reaction to its embarrassing surplusses in the balance of payments. Attempts to encourage the inflows of foreign technology and management but to restrict possibilities for legal control and for excessive rent income have also been applied by Japan. Especially after 1974, with its growing dependence on energy imports, Japan negotiated "product-sharing arrangements" in Indonesia and Saudi Arabia which yield ownership to locals but give the first claim on production to the Japanese. Finally, there are specific domestic policies that heavily influence the location of production. Well-known examples are the bias in American tax laws in favor of foreign direct investment and the restraint on domestic growth of United States antitrust legislation, which encourages companies to expand abroad.

Negative cooperation in investment policies is theoretically conceivable but extremely complex. The functional case for free international capital flows is riddled with difficulties. Government policies, the presence of oligopolies and multisector conglomerates, and complex external factors affecting the choice of location all make it practically impossible to produce an elegant, clear, and persuading case for free international direct investment. Political support for it always depends on the amount of xenophobia in a country.

Liberal investment policies ultimately have implications for trade cooperation. If exports are hampered by trade restrictions, a firm may decide to invest behind the tariff wall, producing inside the protected country and thus avoiding its tariffs. This situation might hurt employment in the firm's home country much more than would a decrease in exports from higher trade barriers. With present low tariff barriers in the OECD area, this effect is not so important for rich countries, but it is for some poor ones. Another effect of liberal investment on trade is in policies toward poor countries. European and Japanese textile investments in semi-industrialized countries tend to generate imports back to the home countries which are highly competitive with domestic textile products and provoke protectionism.

Finally, political concern has recently shifted from international direct investment in the general sense to the specific problem of multinational corporations. Obviously, the distinction between negative and positive cooperation is blurred if cooperation is needed to solve problems related to multinationals. These range from matters of competition and intrafirm international trade to international bribery and the possible withdrawal of companies from South Africa. A well-defined issue area, which is a crucial requirement for successful international cooperation, is missing here. In fact, the eventual implementation of intergovernmental codes will give rise to insoluble questions of jurisdiction.

These two examples from trade and finance point out that negative economic cooperation can no longer be expected to clear the way to the liberal economic order that Charles Kindleberger once called "optimal economic interdependence." This order is characterized by free flows of commodities, productive factors, and technology, with one world money. Instead, the neat split between foreign and domestic policies has been blurred,[22] and the growth of the multinational corporation has created complex linkages between policies within and beyond frontiers.

FORMS OF POSITIVE ECONOMIC COOPERATION

The highest possible form of positive policy cooperation is *unification*. It is defined as the combination of two or more national policy structures into a common one, backed by some form of sanctions. Unification is highly ambitious. It assumes that certain policy areas can be separated from the national government *without* a loss of effectiveness or that federal structures can eventually bind nations into one state. A notorious failure is Western Europe's Common Agricultural Policy. Here the unification of national agricultural policies has remained incomplete. Coercive

[22]Although not treated here, the sensitivity to *demand management* policies in *other* countries has increased so much that they are beginning to become a subject of intergovernmental cooperation that, by nature, cannot be negative! See the section in chap. 3, "Issues of Western Economic Cooperation."

power has been undermined by intergovernmental decision making, which has usurped the authority of the majority, and domestically decided policies still have a critical bearing on the common policy. Western Europe's Common Commercial Policy has recently been quite successful even though it, too, is troubled by the influences of other stabilization policies, especially exchange-rate policy. It nearly goes without saying that to be successful at unification the loyalty to cooperate must not only be positive in spirit but indeed also *self-denying* in character. Policy unification necessarily implies a *fundamental transfer of political responsibility*. But this is an almost prohibitive barrier for modern Western democracies, which have a strong inclination to maintain their own power and reassert themselves.

Coordination involves the internationally negotiated adaptation of domestic policy intentions in order to improve the final impact of these policies for all participants. Coordination is a functional response to economic interdependence, but it is more realistic and modest in its institutional requirements than unification. Policy coordination is concerned with the effectiveness of national policies that are potentially inconsistent in their objectives or conflicting in their instruments. Coordination is based on the explicit recognition that policy making is a domestic process but the affected markets are international and thus the concern of all countries. One may distinguish two types of coordination, *ex ante*, which is anticipatory, and *ex post*, which is responsive.

Ex ante coordination requires a substantial amount of willingness to cooperate, particularly when it is institutionalized. It asserts the rights and power of nations as a group to influence economic policy decisions in other countries *before* the policy has been implemented. Ex ante coordination, as compared with unification, leaves some scope for autonomy in policy because it differs in two basic ways. First, national objectives and priorities are mutually respected as much as possible, and disputes over instruments deal with their intensity rather than the specific mix to be used. Second, the execution of policies is still entirely domestic. The attraction of this second point is somewhat dubious because political responsibility will usually also remain domestic. The problem here is that winning elections and remaining in power presuppose that those elected have, within limits, the means to achieve their programs, and this underlying necessity can be frustrated by ex ante coordination. Of course, in an economically interdependent system the actual room for maneuver is restricted by what is tolerable to one's economic partners, but politicians, interest groups, and voters might favor a different emphasis than that laid down in ex ante coordination. Also, open economies have a greater stake in ex ante coordination than do relatively closed ones, which could give rise to unbalanced and distorted bargaining positions.

In contrast, ex post coordination asks for only modest loyalty, but its effectiveness is questionable. The monetary crises of the last decade have given rise to occasional ex post policy coordination, and the results have been mixed. Can one say that Bonn's refusal to revalue the Deutsche mark in November 1968, despite the encouragement of other OECD members, was a failure of ex post coordination, knowing that one year later the ratio between the French franc and the mark had changed by over 17 percent and the ratio between the dollar and the mark had shifted by 9 percent? Can one say that the Smithsonian Agreement was a successful effort at ex post coordination, knowing that it collapsed 14 months later? In either case, such experiences of ex post coordination seem to have been facilitated and even motivated by the presence of raging crises and threats by some countries to apply beggar-thy-neighbor policies.

Coordination is more often proposed than genuinely pursued! The belief that coordination can result in virtually unchanged policy positions is an illusion because coordination always implies a *serious diminution* of policy autonomy for the governments involved. In some other situations present harmony renders coordination quite superfluous,[23] or the term "coordination" is applied to lower and less sensitive forms of policy cooperation.

Harmonization, for our purposes, comprises efforts to remove

[23] A well-known example is the adoption by the EC Council of Ministers of recommendations about fiscal, monetary, and incomes policy in the middle sixties, when, after the lira crisis of 1963–1964, conditions were quite unproblematic. See Bela Balassa, "Monetary Integration in the European Common

inconsistencies in laws and governmental procedures among co-operating countries. This term can apply to minor technical details of law, to certain systems of interference embodied in law, or to the definition of socioeconomic objectives, instruments, and statistics. Thus, harmonization may vary from a purely functional adjustment of national law to sensitive and politically important issues, such as the definition of a region eligible for financial assistance or the types of agricultural subsidies. It is important to realize that harmonization is *not* the equalization of law but rather the compatibility of law; it is *not* the unification of objectives but the standardization of descriptions of objectives. It does imply identical methods of measurement and therefore the equalization of statistical concepts.

The idea of harmonizing policies rather than legal or institutional procedures can be defended, but some overlap with coordination is hard to avoid. As a way out one may argue that priorities in policy objectives should be harmonized and that the means of attainment should be coordinated. It goes without saying that, in such a complementary conceptualization, national policy autonomy is reduced to the level needed for unification, and thus the combination of harmonization and coordination might meet insurmountable resistance.

Harmonization in its barest form also comes quite close to negative policy cooperation. For example, in harmonizing regional policies, the EC has attempted to make it possible to compare instruments by simply minimizing the types of instruments that could be used. Also, in a similar vein, negotiations about nontariff barriers, such as government procurement policies and aid to industry, involve harmonization because uniform

---

Market," in Bela Balassa (ed.), *European Economic Integration*, North-Holland Publishing Co., Amsterdam, 1975, p. 178. He quotes Raymond Barre as typifying this period as "a climate of false security." During the midseventies, by contrast, EC countries had great problems even paying lip service to macroeconomic policy coordination without any further specification as to contents and constraints. This situation has precluded Tindemans's, and later Duysenberg's, attempt to make all such policies subject to EC Council discussions in order to block further disintegration.

procedures must be set up to evaluate procurement and sectoral aid. But these are part of negative policy cooperation because the goal of such negotiations is to outlaw these trade barriers. In matters of West European integration especially, harmonization has become something of a catchword because it encompasses so much.

Consultation, in this discussion of cooperation, is any exchange and discussion about national policy making that does not imply a commitment on the part of those consulting. As consultation is a typical product of economic interdependence, the frequency of consultative meetings has increased manifold. Consultation guarantees a continuous flow of information and, more important, helps build *confidence*, crucial in a system where every country's acceptance of reduced autonomy depends on other countries doing the same. So the results of consultation cannot be expected to be spectacular, and yet this low-key form of policy cooperation is vital in the OECD economy and even beyond. In rare cases, consultation can be a prelude to informal policy coordination through loose understandings and agreements. Examples can be found in the regular summitry between France and West Germany or perhaps in the Rambouillet, Puerto Rico, London, and Bonn meetings of the heads of state of major First World countries in 1975, 1976, 1977, and 1978, respectively. Similarly, in the Jamaica rewrite of Article IV of the IMF Articles of Agreement, consultation with the Fund is required, at the Fund's request, to ensure compliance with the obligations under Section 1.

There seems to be less clarity with a variety of other terms that are often associated with policy cooperation, such as orchestration, convergence, concertation, or collaboration of policies. In this paper they are all considered equivalent to cooperation.[24]

[24]However, in West European affairs, *concertation* may also denote, according to D. Coombes ("Concertation in the Nation State and in the European Community," in G. Ionescu (ed.), *Between Sovereignty and Integration*, Wiley, New York, 1974, p. 97), "the specific way EC attempts to come to policy decisions via consultation with interest groups and with representatives of national governments for achieving cooperation and consensus in economic

Collaboration has recently attained significance in the "collaboration clause" of the new IMF Article IV, Section 1. This clause has to be interpreted as an official recognition of "a close relationship between domestic and international economic policies."[25] Since a principal objective of the international monetary system is "the continuing development of the orderly underlying conditions that are necessary for financial and economic stability, each member undertakes to collaborate with the Fund and other members to assure orderly exchange arrangements and to promote a stable system of exchange rates."[26]

Finally, something should be said about the international *surveillance* of policies. One might be inclined to think that this term would be indicative of a common policy structure and thus a fairly ambitious form of positive policy cooperation. Such an intuitive classification is surely *not* borne out by cooperation practice. The most well-known example is found in the GATT prescription of multilateral surveillance over unilateral emergency action under Article XIX on market disruption—which is rarely invoked because of its multilateral character and its unpopularity for political reasons. Here we clearly encounter a necessary requirement for successful negative cooperation in trade. Ideally, multilateral surveillance should guarantee that national policies that are harmful to the system as a whole are not applied. The extent to which members fail to invoke multilateral surveillance indicates the limitations of the GATT in monitoring national behavior and fostering negative cooperations.

In the new Article IV, Section 3(b), of the IMF Articles of Agreement, it is stated that "the Fund shall exercise firm surveillance over the exchange rate policies of members."[27] The

---

affairs and . . . [thereby despising] . . . parliamentary methods, which might have presented a direct challenge to the sovereignty of the member states and underlined the political aspects of the decision which were involved." The EC has probably adopted this term from the French *concertation* and the German *Konzertierte Aktion*, which refer to the compatibility of economic plans and stabilization policies with the preferences of business and trade union leaders.

[25] According to the Executive Board of the IMF. See *IMF Survey*, May 2, 1977, p. 131.

[26] *IMF Survey*, January 19, 1976, p. 20.

[27] Ibid.

recent decision on this surveillance is still very general,[28] but it does indicate specific criteria, such as protracted large-scale interventions in one direction on the exchange market and restrictions on trade, money or capital flows, and excessive borrowing. The criteria all point to the fact that the Fund's surveillance is a form of negative cooperation, comparable to that in the GATT. The instrument is informal consultation between the Fund and the member and, ultimately, a report to the Executive Directors. Although the Fund's surveillance is likely to be more efficient than the multilateral surveillance of the GATT, no common policies, harmonization, or coordination are to be expected. The Fund will monitor the system, merely seeing to it that certain conflicting policies are *not* applied.

THE ROLE OF FINANCIAL FUNDS

Financial funds are intergovernmental grants and/or credit facilities that often encourage international economic cooperation. Funds are used for reconstruction, development, commodity stabilization, adjustment of balance-of-payments deficits, and other purposes. Our discussion is limited to international funds of direct relevance to the OECD economy. The most important recent development is the growth and extension of funds as a means for cooperation. Recent examples are the Financial Support Fund of the OECD, the first and second Oil Facility of the IMF, the supplementary Witteveen Facility of the IMF, and the loose commitment of the rich countries in the North-South dialogue to establish an overall Commodity Stabilization Fund.

It is traditionally recognized that funds do not solve many problems but they do help in easing strained systems, in smoothing adjustment, and in preventing or minimizing a deterioration of existing patterns of cooperation. They can also help increase compliance with international rules by combining stricter regulations with the availability of more multilateral finance. This is the accepted practice in the IMF. In the 1960s, the Group of Ten

[28]*IMF Survey*, May 2, 1977, pp. 131–132.

created ad hoc constructions to generate additional borrowing sources for countries that needed to defend their exchange rates. More recent funds have been created in reaction to the vast adjustment problems caused by the oil crisis. They are a response to fears that some countries might attempt to shift some of their adjustment problems to foreigners by competitive devaluations or trade restrictions. The funds offer them the alternative of *slowing down* adjustment rather than *shifting* some of it to other OECD countries with the same adjustment problems.

Thus, funds are another subsidiary instrument for promoting and maintaining reasonable levels of negative economic cooperation. The limits of funds are clear: adjustment cannot be avoided by relying on them, just postponed, and at some point the pain will have to be undergone. For the adjustment between the OECD area and OPEC, this means that reliance on private and public funds must be followed eventually with decreases in oil imports and increases in exports.

Another view on the utility of funds seems to be developing. Funds, or proposals to that effect, are becoming a popular method for governments to show the international community their desire for international economic cooperation *without* materially reducing national autonomy. This is clearest in the EC's tendency to create new funds as lip service to policy cooperation when there is no true basis for harmonization or coordination. When they could not agree on macroeconomic policy coordination to stabilize West European exchange rates, governments refused to admit defeat and established a European Fund for Monetary Cooperation in 1973 that provides only minimal financing and does nothing to produce the needed adjustment. The same goes for the Regional and Social Funds of the EC. Rather than successfully coordinating regional or social policies, they only symbolize progress or buy time for those hardest pressed by adjustment pressures. Furthermore, the vague commitment to a $1 billion Commodity Fund in the North-South dialogue gives the impression of a major concession to poor countries, but it is clear to all observers that such a fund will not affect the structure of the existing international economic order—the basic issue for the South.

Funds are thus a cumbersome and short-term way of dealing with international sensitivities, but they nevertheless are a means of preserving negative policy cooperation. To maintain the international order, increased efforts at cooperation are needed, but a multitude of funds will not perpetually buy off adjustment, national sensitivities, or Third World demands.

THREE

The Future Potential
for Economic Cooperation

The achievements of Western economic cooperation are considerable. Yet, the erosion of trade cooperation and a permissive reform of the monetary system have generated demands for improvements in economic cooperation. Moreover, issue areas that were not covered in the old order, such as international direct investment, are in need of some form of regulation. The increased openness of the OECD economy toward the rest of the world also has induced a series of cooperation demands from non-members. For these reasons, economic cooperation is a highly placed agenda item. In what follows, we will examine the capacity of Western countries to respond positively to these demands and help foster more effective and appropriate cooperation.

ISSUES OF WESTERN ECONOMIC COOPERATION

To get a sense of the range of demands for cooperation, we can classify them according to their ambitiousness.

First, there are a series of demands of a somewhat technical character that do not question the basic nature or scope of the current system of economic cooperation. They arise from the belief that it is the minor imperfections of a basically appropriate system that cause cooperation to falter or be eroded. In the sphere of monetary cooperation, these demands include more regular quota revision, a refinement of the principles of "firm surveillance" over exchange-rate policies, and, perhaps, a greater role for SDRs as opposed to dollars and gold. In trade cooperation, these demands take in a technical reform of the GATT on such points as using import controls for balance-of-payments purposes (Article XII) and resorting to emergency action when rapid import growth disrupts markets (Article XIX). Some of these issues deal with the adequacy of multilateral surveillance and are likely to be negotiated seriously. Unlike other more sensitive issues of economic cooperation, improved international regulation in these matters will only marginally influence domestic politics, and thus a functional approach to their settlement is quite possible.

Second, a number of demands have been made that would widen substantially the scope of economic cooperation without changing the nature of intergovernmental economic management. These demands grow out of the belief that, rather than technical shortcomings, it is the incomplete coverage of issue areas that undermines current economic cooperation. In the monetary sphere, this means supervising the Euro-currency and Euro-capital markets or making rules on flows of short-term capital or portfolio investment. In the microeconomic sphere the demands include the harmonization of certain nontariff distortions, a more severe regulation of agricultural trade to suppress cavalier protectionism in that sector, the inclusion of negative cooperation and multilateral surveillance in export controls, and the regulation of international direct investment policies.

These proposals are clearly more ambitious than the technical ones. They are likely to require more cooperation than most countries can or will provide. Some proposals are simply beyond current capacity for cooperation, and in other cases domestic concerns prevail which create barriers to successful negotiation. The regulation of the Euro-currency market is frustrated because the capacities of most governments for cooperation are not equal to the task. Nontariff distortions are hard to negotiate because it is difficult to compare concessions. Countries are also reluctant to give up domestic political autonomy over government procurement. They can be expected to reach agreement on a loose OECD Code of Government Procurement, but it remains to be seen how much a code would alter governmental behavior.

The regulation of international direct investment has been approached only symbolically through several nonmandatory codes of conduct.[29] Here it is both the inability to cooperate and domestic political unwillingness that hamper progress. Other, far-reaching proposals in the investment field also get little support. This is the case with the American desire to internationalize antitrust policies. In general, a widening of scope will have little chance of success except maybe in the case of export controls. Unlike the other proposals, the latter entails a definite problem of negative cooperation on well-defined issues in a limited number of sectors.

Third, a number of analysts, but very few government officials, have concluded that the future viability of international economic cooperation hinges on a broad array of new techniques and instruments that would change the nature of cooperation. This position is usually based on the view that economic cooperation is eroded and incomplete and that dissatisfaction with it cannot be contained indefinitely. There are several proposals, but we shall confine ourselves to two examples.

The first one is the call for positive cooperation in macroeconomic policies, as suggested by Marina v. N. Whitman. She holds that the United States is in a good position to lead the way toward positive cooperation. "Certainly, the effort must be made; both the logic of analysis and the evidence from recent experiences indicate that, despite the partial buffer provided by managed flexibility of exchange rates, tension persists between the vulnerability created by increasing market integration and the fragmentation of policy formation. If we do not find ways to coordinate policies, we will inevitably slip backward from market integration."[30] The best way to contain the erosion of negative cooperation, so the argument runs, is to transcend it and establish

---

[29]In 1977 the International Chamber of Commerce (ICC), the International Labor Organization (ILO), and the OECD produced such codes, with a difference in emphasis. The European Parliament (of the EC) and the United States Congress were in the process of producing a joint code. The UN hoped to agree on a code in 1978.

[30]Whitman, "Sustaining the International Economic System," p. 27.

positive forms of cooperation. The EC experience shows, however, that even unequivocal political commitments made in well-publicized EC summit declarations could not generate the will to complete the first stage of the plan for a European Economic and Monetary Union. The EC conditions at that time, in 1971, were far more conducive to cooperation than OECD conditions are likely to be in the medium-term future.

The EC has been able to create and sustain a Common Agricultural Policy (CAP), a unique precedent of unification, be it at great economic and bureaucratic costs. In addition, it was in the process of completing a Common Commercial Policy, had already established a customs union, and was attempting to negotiate on non-tariff distortions (NTDs), though these efforts have been frustrated in recent years. The EC has a variety of committees on macroeconomic policy making, for both the short and medium terms. By 1977, the "snake" arrangement—an effort to maintain pegged exchange rates among members and thus float as a group—had been in jeopardy for five years and was reduced to an ever smaller group pegged to the Deutsche mark. However, the snake is the one symbol that remains from the moderate first stage of the Monetary Union. Even the tightly knit Benelux countries have had a hard time trying to maintain a narrow band around the announced guilder-franc ratio, an arrangement slightly more ambitious than the snake. These bad experiences have slowed the dynamics of integration in Western Europe, which in itself makes OECD cooperation harder. If anything, however, it dims the prospects for positive cooperation in a much looser, more differentiated "affluent alliance." The OECD lacks the pressure for macroeconomic policy convergence and does not require the fixed exchange rates needed for the CAP and the customs union. It also lacks the bureaucratic machinery and optimism for building such intense cooperation.

Positive cooperation is also problematic because the lower stages of it are obscure. Higher stages, such as unification or ex ante coordination, are well-known but must be preceded by less ambitious efforts, creating the atmosphere for further transfers of authority. Whitman distinguishes two forms. "The most limited form of positive coordination, wherein each country takes account of the probable policies of others in setting its own, is clearly essential to avoid the global inflationary or deflationary 'overkill.' "[31] Although the purpose is clear here, the procedure is vague, which may well be the cause for failure. Further on, she refers to this lower phase as "intensified consultation," giving little guarantee of success.[32] The series of economic summits at Rambouillet, Puerto Rico, and London in 1975–1977 can be defined as intensified consultation strengthened by dialogue within the OECD. The actual impact of these summits has been weak, however. In 1976–1977, West Germany and Japan were not prepared to spur effective demand, fearing renewed inflation. It thus became even harder for OECD economies with feeble currencies to prevent further depreciations and obtain foreign exchange with which to pay for oil imports. Also, the trade deficit of the United States in 1977 was a result of petroleum imports and concealed a trade surplus with many OECD partners.

Whitman's second stage is described more clearly, but it is even more demanding: "A framework within which nations actually agree on broad macro-economic targets and plan policies to achieve them cooperatively, including the coordination of policy timetables."[33] This stage requires far more readiness to cooperate than OECD governments, including the United States, can muster at this time.

The second proposal for changing the nature of intergovernmental economic management by John Pinder, is concerned with radically different instruments for microeconomic cooperation. We have noted before that the theoretical model of negative cooperation in trade and investment contrasts sharply with the tendency of Western governments to intervene in the economy by making adjustments smoother and slower or influencing the composition of output and employment. In a provocative paper, Pinder made a case for a regulated international trade system rather than a liberal one.

[31]Whitman, op. cit., p. 23.
[32]Ibid.
[33]Ibid.

In trade, the international policy system is still based on the laissez faire ideal of free trade with the minimum of exceptions. This divergence between domestic and international economic management is dangerous; for the new domestic economic management responds to real needs and, where it conflicts with the international system, it will usually win. . . . Sooner or later, but preferably sooner, the international system will have to be revised to incorporate the durable principles of the new domestic economic management. Otherwise, trade will be the victim of an expanding domestic policy system at odds with a contracting international system.[34]

He favors the replacement of free trade by the controlled growth of imports, especially those from less developed countries, supplemented with international supervision and adjustment assistance. In addition, appropriate reciprocity is required in East-West trade negotiations.[35] He argues that trade negotiations on primary products "should take as a starting point the degree of self-sufficiency . . . and the need to agree on a high level of stocks . . . against disruption due to shortage, instead of being confused by an assumption that reasonable people should be seeking laissez faire and free trade."[36] He also goes as far as approving publicly supported international cartels for capital-intensive industries in times of recession.[37] His final point is that "it is the multinational companies that have the clearest interest in such reforms," for several reasons, but notably because "doctrinal laissez faire is . . . alien to their methods of management. They seek secure supplies of materials at stable prices; apply manpower development not hire-and-fire-policies; take a long view of their investments and nurse weaker sections through difficult patches."[38]

[34]John Pinder, "Towards a New System of International Economic Management," paper presented to a colloquium of the Atlantic Institute, December 1976 (mimeo), pp. 8–9.

[35]Pinder proposes to exchange a lowering of trade barriers for Eastern European products for investment commitments in noncompeting products by Council for Mutual Economic Assistance (Comecon) countries.

[36]Pinder, p. 4.

[37]Ibid., p. 5. In May 1978, the EC Commissioner for Competition Policy, Mr. Vouël, announced proposals to be submitted to the EC Council of Ministers about a circumscribed form of "crisis cartels."

[38]Ibid., p. 11.

Two objections immediately come to mind. The first one is the great danger that political tension will build up in this system because of mutual accusations of mercantilism and the inability to control misconduct, creating an atmosphere that magnifies conflicts and frustrates negotiation. The main objective of this system might be "the stable growth of trade and production,"[39] but cooperation is bound to be unstable because all the distinct elements of domestic politics have such pervasive influence on economic policy.

A second objection is against the tight cooperation between multinationals and governments. For socialists and other progressive parties in Western Europe, far-reaching government participation in international production cartels and quota agreements is ideologically hard to digest. For them these measures would require a firmer governmental grip on companies that are members of the cartels. However, more extensive government controls would certainly mean a major shift in these countries toward planned economies. This is a move that will generate staunch opposition, as can be seen by the experience of the French Left with nationalization. On the other hand, if governments take a passive stance toward the approval of these international cartels of multinational firms, problems of control and jurisdiction will develop because there is no international body that can effectively regulate the behavior of multinationals. We would have the worst of all possible worlds: during a recession the cartel might be unstable and collapse, and in a recovery it might be so strong that it would be impossible to control by OECD-wide organs.

In brief, while I respect some of the merits of Pinder's proposal, it makes demands that are far in excess of the present capacities of OECD countries to cooperate.

THE GLOBAL CONNECTION

It is not my purpose to open up the North-South debate or examine the economic side of détente. For our purposes, it will suffice to speak in general terms about some major implications

[39]Ibid., p. 12.

that the structure of global economic relations has for intergovernmental cooperation in the OECD area.

In the 1940s and 1950s, there was little merit in considering the total set of international economic relations as a world economy. The European socialist countries were nearly autarkic as a group, and China only very marginally participated in international commerce. Also the periphery, consisting of colonies and underdeveloped economies highly dependent on the West for technology and exports of raw materials, was subservient to the core group of economies—the countries now in the OECD. The world economy, therefore, consisted of a fairly closed system of economic relations among OECD countries with controlled and secure access to the raw materials of the periphery. Given the security of supplies from the periphery, Western countries could concentrate on building their export markets through negative economic cooperation. Thus, the management of the world economy was largely reduced to the promotion of negative economic cooperation in the OECD area and the controlled cultivation of supplies from the periphery. Both in the West and at the periphery, this management was fairly effective.

At the periphery, efficacy was a product of the hierarchical nature of the world economy. The OECD area dominated the periphery through its economic size and power, which was manifested, for example, in the weighted voting of the IMF, shipping conferences, the restricted availability of technology, and the dominance of multinational enterprises. This asymmetry grew out of the unbalanced dependence of the periphery on the West as a market for its exports and the relative insignificance of these links for the Western countries.

As the 1980s approach, the world economy seems to be moving painfully toward a hexagonal structure. The political reorientation from bipolarity to multipolarity will further increase East-West trade and Western "industrial cooperation," akin to direct investment, with Eastern Europe. The recent involvement of China in world politics has been followed by a rapid growth in its international economic relations. The end of formal colonialism and the call for economic development have complicated the OECD-area relationship with the periphery. The periphery has gradually come to be divided into a hopelessly unfortunate Fourth World, a slowly industrializing Third World, and a relatively powerful and determined group of petroleum-rich countries. For the 1980s, this means a highly complex world economy in which the Western countries will have to manage their economic relations with five different groups: the Third and Fourth Worlds, OPEC, China, and Comecon. All five are distinct in character, political preferences, and stage of economic development; thus, the efficiency of world economic management is further complicated and its success is severely threatened.

The economic relations of the Western countries with these five different groups do not begin to compare with the elegant implicit logic or strenuous organization of traditional Western cooperation. East-West cooperation is simply badly organized. The OECD and Comecon do not talk on a regular basis, the EC is still not fully recognized by Comecon, and there is no systematic relationship between Comecon and the GATT or the IMF. Relations with China are hardly through the first stage of trade missions and ad hoc exports. Ties with OPEC are in the process of being structured in the EC-Arabian dialogue and in discussions between North and South. Most OPEC countries, however, are not GATT members and their relation to the IMF is confusing, especially given their great financial strength and low levels of development.

Relations with the Third and Fourth Worlds are ambiguous. On the one hand, there is the tendency to cooperate on a continent-by-continent basis: the United States with Latin America, the EC with Africa, and Japan with Southeast Asia. The foremost example of this cooperation is the Lomé Agreement between the EC and nearly all African and some Caribbean countries, concluded in 1975. On the other hand, there is a genuine lack of consensus on the demands for a New International Economic Order (NIEO), reflected in the Conference on International Economic Cooperation (CIEC) and in the UN General Assembly, ECOSOC and UNCTAD.

The NIEO has raised issues that will be an integral part of diplomatic talks on global economic cooperation for decades to come. NIEO demands, such as an integrated commodity price-stabilization fund, the internationally agreed transfer of older industries to poor countries, the international indexation of commodity prices, and enforced technology transfers conflict with the existing economic order. They are likely to be seen as excessive demands, apart from the issue of their appropriateness. Moreover, for many poor countries, the NIEO is more political than economic, in the sense that bloc voting in the UN and ostentatious declarations by groups of poor countries are the only way they have of visibly pressuring Western decision making. In contrast, the continental approach to North-South relations is more likely to produce effective commitments and provide funds, indicating the relevant direction of cooperation with the poor world.

THE DECLINE OF MULTILATERAL MANAGEMENT

Besides looking at the substance of economic cooperation in the OECD and global settings, we can also assess the present capacity and willingness of OECD members to cooperate by observing some institutional trends. In this connection, the effectiveness of Western economic cooperation is likely to be influenced by the growing importance of hierarchical and regional cooperation as well as through horizontal extensions of cooperation.

The rise of hierarchical decision making in policy cooperation is not surprising. What is peculiar is the belated reappearance of it after some two decades of undisputed United States leadership. With the emergence of Japan as a great economic power, the stagnation of the EC, and the decline of United States economic dominance, patterns of cooperation have evolved accordingly. Decisions on major principles of cooperation are now made by an elite group of First World countries, presumably to avoid a broader, more cumbersome multilateral process of policy cooperation. The desire to exclude certain countries is a modest attempt at using the leverage of power in foreign policy and is, therefore, liable to produce strains within the First World if pushed too far.

Regional policy cooperation is of course not new, but it no longer seems to be framed in a global perspective. The formation and accentuation of economic blocs have been said to be the wave of the future.[40] For example, one can envisage a fragmentation of the First World into three economic blocs—the EC, a North American bloc, and a Pacific bloc. There are several difficulties with this vision. Conceptually, North America is only a tandem in which Canada will continue to take part in a system of negative policy cooperation whose profits, industrial structure, wages, and use of resources are determined largely by the American market. In a similar vein, the Pacific bloc, too, seems remote. Even if it did develop, it would have to include various less developed countries along with Japan and the Australian–New Zealand customs union in a complex arrangement, somewhat comparable to the EC's approach to Mediterranean and African countries. Only the EC fits the notion of an economic bloc and will stand alone for some time to come. Thus, although economic tripolarization is frequently mentioned, it does not refer to three economic blocs but rather to an odd hybrid of the United States, Japan, and the EC.

Both regional and hierarchical cooperation can create obstacles to other forms of cooperation, undermining the multilateral framework. Hierarchical cooperation among the largest economies forces them to impose similar agreements on neighboring, economically dependent countries for the sake of consistency. Although this does work sometimes, it is sure to irritate relations between large and small countries. There is no current mechanism for imposing policy cooperation, and the odds are that such a mechanism would be either impossible to build or counterproductive. So when the tension between the two generates a lot of discord, the offended nation must be appeased to calm relations and maintain a cooperative atmosphere. For example, when Canada was irritated because it was not considered a core country, it was bought off by being included in the Puerto Rico summit.

[40]See E. M. Preeg, *Economic Blocs and U.S. Foreign Policy*, report 35, National Planning Association, Washington, D. C., 1974, and R. Gilpin, *U.S. Power and the Multinational Corporation*, Basic Books, New York, 1975, chaps. III and IX.

Similarly, the EC was represented at the London meetings mainly to conciliate the Benelux countries.

This argument would be irrelevant if the Big Seven could somehow take up the old United States role of economic leadership in the First World, instituting financial facilities and granting concessions and specific aid that nullify resistance to the imposed order. However, there is little prospect for unified common leadership because it is beyond the reach of summits. The utility of hierarchical policy cooperation is therefore limited. It can, however, be an adequate method for coping with a threatening crisis or with deadlocks in low-key functional negotiations on policy cooperation. The Rambouillet meeting, for example, stimulated a breakthrough in international monetary negotiations, and the London summit attempted to enhance the Multilateral Trade Negotiations. However, the vagueness and looseness of hierarchical cooperation in summits inhibit the strengthening of economic policy cooperation. The regularity of economic summits—a process institutionalized within the EC—is clear evidence that national economic security is a highly significant political preference that depends on a minimal level of international cooperation, but because it is so politically sensitive, cooperation cannot easily be pushed beyond the mere preservation of economic interdependence as it now stands.

Regional policy cooperation tends to enhance economic openness among the cooperating countries while diminishing openness toward third countries. This fact is illustrated by the operations of a customs union such as the EC since 1968. After intraunion tariffs are eliminated and a common outer tariff is set up, intraunion trade increases for three reasons: because of trade creation, trade diversion, and income growth.[41] By contrast, the

---

[41]Trade is created by the removal of barriers between member countries. Trade is diverted from third countries to member countries to the extent that the higher prices charged for goods by firms in member countries are outweighed by the burden of the common external, tariff, which must be paid when relying on non–customs union suppliers of these goods. Finally, the increased income resulting from the growth of trade adds to the imports of member countries, further increasing intraunion trade.

union's trade with third countries declines because of trade diversion and is not influenced by trade creation. It increases solely in some proportion to income growth. Thus, bloc formation reflects a desire to cooperate within the group which is different in degree and kind from the loyalty to cooperate with third parties.

Policy cooperation with third countries is secondary in the context of regional policy cooperation. In a bloc, there is more resistance to pursuing externally conflicting policies, implying protracted and comprehensive negotiations on external matters, such as the Multilateral Trade Negotiations. Realizing this, third countries often fear bloc formation except when it increases their national security. This fear of blocs can lead to a strategy of undermining the cohesion and progress of regional cooperation by promoting hierarchical cooperation, which divides the large and small economies in the bloc.

The horizontal extension of economic cooperation refers to a reluctance to engage in commitments that intensify cooperation; instead the goal is to use various means to prevent falling back to lower levels of cooperation. Horizontal extensions attempt to reconcile domestic political needs for economic security with the functional requirements necessary for preserving the present level of economic interdependence. Today a flat refusal to engage in consultation is uncommon, but it is also rare for most talks to produce genuinely effective commitments. The multiplicity of financial funds in the EC, the OECD, and the UN testify to this urge for unproductive compromise. Economic summits that merely produce powerless communiqués or new agencies, such as the International Energy Agency, that barely have constitutions are also examples of horizontal extensions of cooperation. In the EC-Arabian dialogue and the North-South discussions, package deals are endlessly discussed, but the talks have little more than symbolic value.

There are dangers in these horizontal extensions of cooperation. Not only are they tiring and bound to generate inconsistencies, but they also have natural limits. The growing number of these international economic organizations complicates cooperation and dilutes its results because membership, financial contributions, functions, and authority are never identical but are also rarely completely separate or reconcilable. Therefore, the desire to cooperate remains hesitant and negative, continuously producing the need for ad hoc new agreements to contain the system's inconsistencies.

Hierarchical, regional, and horizontal economic cooperation have generated a glut of conferences, sessions, and summits about economic cooperation but at the same time have yielded few, if any, improvements in economic cooperation. As a group, they seem to provide the instruments necessary for system maintenance in the absence of a firmly structured international economy.

CONCLUSIONS

The foreseeable future is no time for neat models and grand designs. The substantial influence of domestic politics on market processes and especially the multilevel search for economic security have slowly eroded the postwar structure of Western economic cooperation and limited the prospects for effective improvements in multilateral economic management. Furthermore, the transition to a hexagonal world economy is far from complete. Its ultimate effects on economic relations are unknown and perhaps cannot be dealt with by the low-key, ad hoc forms of cooperation that prevail at present. In the medium term, perhaps well into the 1980s, demands on the OECD area for group cooperation with the rest of the world are likely to be handled with great reluctance.

The basic underlying issue for the OECD economies will be the search for economic security internationally, nationally, and individually. Given present levels of national welfare and degree of interdependence among the OECD nations, a major recurring theme will necessarily be the preservation of negative economic cooperation. Preservation is in itself feasible, but its success will be threatened by the need to adjust to the greater openness of the OECD economy, especially with respect to energy consumption and traditional industries. Therefore, the management of this adjustment will be crucial to the objective of system maintenance. However, the prospects for an orderly adjustment to the imports from industrializing countries are discouraging. The nearly prohibitive barriers to positive policy cooperation, on the one hand, and the absence of any cooperative mechanisms for an adequate regulation of international trade growth, on the other, do not bode well for OECD-area adjustment.

With Western economic cooperation hinging on the willingness of all sides to reduce policy autonomy, the further erosion of negative economic cooperation is likely to be destabilizing. Thus, it is indispensable to first solve the adjustment problems within the OECD area. Doing this need not be as cumbersome as some people think.

The three most crucial elements of internal adjustment are the Japanese export drive, the rise of the Mediterranean economies, and the differing burdens imposed by oil imports. The rapid increases in Japanese exports to the United States and recently to Western Europe have directly affected the Europeans in only a few small subsectors—bearings and certain parts of shipbuilding. These have been accommodated by voluntary export restraints and by intense EC-Japanese negotiations to facilitate European exports to Japan. The problem of Japanese exports to the United States will have to be resolved in a similar way. Trade diplomats tend to ignore market accommodation to the threat of insecure market access. When, in 1970–1971, the United States Congress was debating the Burke-Hartke bill, export-replacing direct investments were made in the United States by Japanese firms. Also, the recent call for protectionism in Western Europe seems to have induced increases in Japanese direct investment. Obviously, foreign direct investments in the form of new productive capacity greatly reduce the employment losses in less competitive industries that would result from increased imports. This factor might, for example, brighten the dark long-run prospects for automobile production in Europe.

The rise of the Mediterranean economies is being taken care of optimally given the circumstances. Portugal, Spain, and Greece are attempting to become full members of the EC. There are some political grounds for membership, but nevertheless the negotiations will be difficult. This very sensitive adjustment problem within the OECD economy is best resolved within the relatively effective regional framework for trade cooperation that the EC possesses. An EC failure to incorporate these three countries will mean even sharper conflicts with other semi-industrialized countries that ask for market access in the future.

The burden of petroleum imports is very unevenly distributed. The problem is exacerbated by exchange-rate depreciations. Sharp devaluations do eventually encourage greater exports, but not when the entire OECD economy grows so slowly. In addition, a devaluation increases the cost of all imports, further augmenting the oil bill in terms of stable currencies. These same influences also disrupt the economies of oil and gas exporters in the OECD area, such as Canada, Great Britain, Norway, and the Netherlands. Their currencies appreciate because of their improved trading position, causing further unemployment in their export sectors. Here OECD economies will have to adjust on an individual basis to OPEC countries, especially by increasing their exports to the oil producers. Moderate optimism with respect to total export growth seems warranted given the experience of the period since 1973.

This leads to a final general point on the openness of the OECD economy to the rest of the world. The long-run adjustment to the greater openness of the OECD economy is eventually going to be facilitated by rising exports, first to the OPEC countries and later to other industrializing countries. The relevance of this point is small for the medium term, providing little consolation for the 1980s. It is a functional observation not concerned with the enforced adjustment problems of the transition period, which will last until the flow of goods into the OECD is matched by OECD export flows. Thus, for the medium term, the preservation of the achievements of negative economic cooperation in this unstable environment is a critical challenge for the Western countries.

Selected Bibliography

Camps, Miriam: "First World Relationships: The Role of the OECD," *Council Papers on International Affairs*, no. 5, Council on Foreign Relations, New York, 1975.

Coombes, D.: "Concertation in the Nation State and in the European Community," in G. Ionescu (ed.), *Between Sovereignty and Integration*, Wiley, New York, 1974.

Cooper, Richard N.: *The Economics of Interdependence*, McGraw-Hill for the Council on Foreign Relations, New York, 1968.

———: "Trade Policy Is Foreign Policy," reprinted in Richard Cooper (ed.), *A Reordered World*, Potomac Association, Washington, D.C., 1973.

———: "Worldwide vs. Regional Integration: Is There an Optimum Size of the Integrated Area?" in Fritz Machlup (ed.), *Economic Integration Worldwide, Regional, Sectoral*, Macmillan, London, 1976.

Dornbusch, Rudiger, and Krugman, Paul: "Flexible Exchange Rates in the Short Run," *Brookings Papers on Economic Activity*, vol. 7, no. 3, The Brookings Institution, Washington, D.C., 1976, pp. 531–566.

Fellner, William (ed.): *Contemporary Economic Problems 1977*, American Enterprise Institute for Public Policy Research, Washington, D. C., 1977.

Friedman, Milton: "The Role of Monetary Policy," *American Economic Review*, vol. 58, March 1968, pp. 1–17.

———, et al. *Milton Friedman's Monetary Framework: A Debate with His Critics*, University of Chicago Press, Chicago, 1974.

Gilpin, Robert: *U.S. Power and the Multinational Corporation*, Basic Books, New York, 1975.

Gordon, Robert J.: *Macroeconomics*, Little-Brown, Boston, 1978.

———: "Recent Developments in the Theory of Inflation and Unemployment," *Journal of Monetary Economics*, vol. 2, April 1976, pp. 185–219.

———: "The Demand for and Supply of Inflation," *Journal of Law and Economics*, vol. 18, December 1975, pp. 807–836.

Hirsch, F., and Doyle, M.: "Politicization in the World Economy: Necessary Conditions for an International Economic Order," in F. Hirsch, M. Doyle, and E. Morse, *Alternatives to Monetary Disorder*, McGraw-Hill for the Council on Foreign Relations/1980s Project, New York, 1977.

Katzenstein, Peter: "International Relations and Domestic Structures: Foreign Economic Policies of Advanced Industrial States," *International Organization*, vol. 30, no. 1, winter 1976.

Kindleberger, Charles: "Optimal Economic Interdependence," in Charles Kindleberger and Andrew Shonfield (eds.), *North American and Western European Economic Policies*, Macmillan, London, 1971.

Lindbeck, Assar: "Stabilization Policy in Open Economies with Endogenous Politicians," *American Economic Review*, vol. 66, May 1976, pp. 1–19.

Modigliani, Franco: "The Monetarist Controversy, Or, Should We Forsake Stabilization Policy?" *American Economic Review*, vol. 67, March 1977, pp. 1–19.

Okun, Arthur M.: "Fiscal-Monetary Activism: Some Analytical Issues," *Brookings Papers on Economic Activity*, vol. 3, The Brookings Institution, Washington, D.C., 1972, pp. 123–163.

Preeg, Ernest: *Economic Blocs and U.S. Foreign Policy*, report 135, National Planning Association, Washington, D.C., 1974.

Stein, Jerome M. (ed.): *Monetarism*, North-Holland Publishing Co., Amsterdam, 1976.

Tinbergen, Jan, et al.: *Reshaping the International Order: A Report to the Club of Rome*, Dutton, New York, 1976.

Tobin, James: "Keynesian Models of Recession and Depression," *American Economic Review*, vol. 65, May 1975, pp. 195–202.

Whitman, Marina v. N.: "Sustaining the International Economic System: Issues for U.S. Policy," *Essays in International Finance*, no. 121, Princeton University, Princeton, N.J., June 1977.

Index

About the Authors

ROBERT J. GORDON is currently professor of economics at Northwestern University and a research associate of the National Bureau of Economic Research. In addition to many other professional activities, Professor Gordon has been, since 1970, affiliated with the Brookings Panel on Economic Activity and has served in several capacities as an economic advisor to the U.S. government. He has published numerous articles in U.S. journals and contributed to various books on macroeconomics. Professor Gordon is also the author of the text *Macroeconomics* and the editor of *Milton Friedman's Monetary Framework: A Debate with His Critics*. He studied at Harvard and Oxford, and has a doctorate from M.I.T.

JACQUES PELKMANS is assistant professor of international economics at Tilburg University in the Netherlands. He has also taught at the Dutch Association for International Affairs, the Netherlands School of Business, and Northern Illinois University. He was a Fulbright-Hays Research Fellow and has published several articles in Dutch periodicals. His current research interests include foreign direct investment, European economic integration, and the future of foreign trade policy. Professor Pelkmans received his Ph.D. in 1975 from Tilburg University.

EDWARD L. MORSE is Special Assistant in the Office of the Under Secretary for Economic Affairs, Department of State. He was formerly Executive Director of the 1980s Project of the Council on Foreign Relations.

THOMAS E. WALLIN, associate editor of the 1980s Project of the Council on Foreign Relations, received his master's degree in 1977 from Columbia University, School of International Affairs.